MW01618304

Praise for **The Dance Between Hope & Fear**, John's first book

Here is a story of compassion, experience, vocation and courage. Not one to curse the darkness, John Calvi seeks, and spreads, light, overcoming fear and tribulation with hope and faith. An irresistible combination of common sense, grounded humour, wit and storytelling, with much to ponder. This book is a must read for anyone with a love of humanity in their heart.

John Punshon - professor, Earlham School of Religion

John Calvi once counseled that the time had arrived for me to step out into 'thin air.' How right he was. May Calvi's wisdom and vast experience free many others to move from darkness into the light. In an era drenched in fear, his clarity frees us to find our courage."

Frances Moore Lappé - founder, Small Planet Institute

This is a retrospective collection of disparate essays, poems, deep reflections, recipes, and even some original music, by a very special individual who has spent the past three decades of his life providing massage therapy to people often suffering from overwhelming physical or psychological needs. Calvi has been able to overcome his own occasionally arising doubts and self-perceived shortcomings to find the continuing strength to carry on this mission through so many years, having discovered his inner light that led him to the Quaker faith. Regardless of their ability to pay, Calvi has been bringing succor especially to those who had been variously traumatized or were victims of AIDS or other serious illness. Although arranged into eight somewhat chronological sections, the many included pieces are sufficiently independent of each other so that one can dip into the book almost at random for insights, inspiration, and even occasional humor. I was especially impressed by Calvi's contributions to the "Quaker Initiative to End Torture", especially by our own country via the CIA.

Arthur H. Westing - Prof Emeritus of Environmental Sciences

Calvi is a Quaker healer. And though he might quail at the term, I would also call him a practical Quaker theologian.

He's a practical theologian because, for more than twenty years, he has been both practicing, and learning from the practice. On the one hand, he heals the sick (or at least eases their pain), comforts the dying, and helps bring rest to the stressed and exhausted (i.e., practically everyone else). He began developing this gift as a ministry as the worldwide AIDS plague struck, then followed it through the homegrown plagues of war and torture.

On another hand, Calvi is a theologian because he has had considerable dealings with angels, plus visitations from Jesus, Mary and, lest he become overly sectarian, Buddha. And then on a third hand (a bow to the Trinitarians?) he thinks and writes about it all – which of course is the dead-giveaway sign of being a theologian. In fact, he's been thinking and writing about all this for years.

His first book, The Dance Between Hope & Fear, brought together some of these stray writings, and was most welcome. This new one extends his work and witness further. Let us hope there's still more to come.

Chuck Fager - Editor, Quaker Theology Summer-(Fall 2013, Issue #23)

I have two copies of your book. One to keep safe in my library and one to lend out to friends whom I deem worthy of The Gospel According to St. John. The work (the book) and the work (your life) are truly inspiring. You have articulated both with love, courage, empathy, and great skill.

Peter L. DalNegro – former Head, Renbrook Upper School

When your book came, I kept opening it at random. The sampling was so rich I was late to a commitment, not talking a bit late either. Created a lot of interest in what kept me as I went on and on with enthusiasm. Going to be some book orders among other healers. Then there was resentment day when I did not have an opportunity read. Now I am reading it, digesting, rereading, digesting & profoundly moved. I am enjoying the masterful balance of diving down into the dark & then coming back up.

Thank you John for this amazing gift. Love the idea of cd and future volumes.

Cherly Clemmensen – Bioacoustic Research Associate Sound Health Options

This is a beautiful account of healing, redemption, the dark places in our own hearts and the brilliance that more often than not finds us and claims us. John is a teacher, guide and participant in the dance he describes. He writes with candor, tenderness and humor. It is such a beautiful and real account of his own journey to heal and the journey he makes everyday to heal others. As a body worker/healer, John's powerful book reminds me of why I do the work I do. His words are meaningful to everyone.

Tim Rogers - massage therapist and holistic body worker, Washington DC

If you ever wondered what it is like to heal your own pain and that of others, this book tells you. It is a powerful journey through, not around or avoiding, life's heavy lessons, both for the healer-author and for the thousands of others he has helped.

Sas Carey - energy healer, filmmaker, and author of *Reindeer Herders in My Heart.*

John Calvi is one of those rare creatures that seem to bring peace with them wherever they go. If you haven't had the chance to be with him in person, the next best thing is being with his thoughtful, lighthearted and sensitive writing.

Roland Tec - filmmaker *We Pedal Uphill, Defiance, All the Rage*

John Calvi's touch is warm and sure. He gives peace and certainty in times of great fear and brokenness and pain. His IS a healing touch. John's writing in "The Dance Between Hope and Fear" evokes the

Friendly humor, centeredness, and outrageous presence that he offers in person. It is a book to keep under your pillow.

Tom Hoskins M.D., Putney Friends Meeting

While reading *The Dance Between Hope & Fear*, I found myself jotting down some of Calvi's insights to use in the Discerning Our Calls class I teach at Pendle Hill. A few examples: our callings are not so much about changing the world as changing ourselves and growing closer to the Divine; a little fear is a good thing in a calling, but you have to pay attention to how much fear you can handle; "no love is ever wasted," even if the patient dies, or gets deported back to the country where he was tortured; you know your ministry is mature when you can serve with compassion the fool in your meeting "who just fries your butt." Many of his wisdoms are simple points that resonate deeply.

At the core of Calvi's story is a deep trust that he'll be given what he needs when he needs it. Like the journals of early Friends who lived in radical obedience to divine guidance, this book can encourage contemporary Friends in our struggles to do the same.

Eileen Flanagan – author - *Renewable: One Woman's Search for Simplicity, Faithfulness, and Hope.* Friends Journal Book Review Nov 2013

Praise for John's hands-on work and teaching

I'd rather like to say a bit about John Calvi's caring. I have stage four cancer and suffer with a lot of pain. The pain I have I acknowledge will most likely never be fully relieved. The closest I have ever been to full release from my suffering was the week I was "treated" by John. John doesn't just use his hands but manages to be a point of energy collection and transfer bringing a relief that is greater than just the relief of the physical pain. Pain is much more than the physical feeling we suffer and John was able to help me with relief far beyond my physical suffering. I only wish I could have been with him more than a week.

Carter Nash – Homeless Advocate and Active Quaker

For many years I found the healing miracles something of a problem. I simply didn't believe them.

Knowing John, and having experienced myself the healing power in his hands, I have come to understand more clearly how Jesus healed. It is by a transfer of power and energy from the healer to the person being healed. It requires in the healer the willingness to be involved in another's suffering, and also the willingness to be drained or used up. "The power has gone out of me," said Jesus. It is exhausting work, and from time to time the healer is in need of healing. It requires in the person being healed faith that the healing can take place, active participation, and a sense of selfhood and self-worthy: the conviction that one's life is important and worthy of being brought back to wholeness."

Elizabeth G. Watson - Quaker feminist theologian, author *Wisdom's Daughters Stories of the Women Around Jesus* 1997, page 51 – 52

John Calvi's weekends are restorative. This is, in large part, due to who John is. Spirit goes with John and people can sense Spirit even if they can't name it. He is grounded and centered, an extension of that Divine Love and there is a sense of calm and peace. John does a lot of what I would call life teaching – offering ways to live and work in the world without burn-out. Wouldn't it be great to carry less tension, fatigue, and worry?

John teaches in a variety of ways – he demonstrates massage and energy work using his calm presence and voice, encouraging us to offer this gift to another. During the questions and clarifications times, he teaches by storytelling, drawing upon the countless interactions with his spouse, family, friends and workshop participants. His use of humor often lessens the tension in the room and allows the learning to go deeper for those who are open to it. Friends learn in a non-threatening, non-judgmental way.

John uses his intuitive gifts, picking up trauma, tension, fatigue in another. He'll often lay his hand on a shoulder, sending healing Light without any fanfare. The person feels safe and cared for. At other times, he'll call a person out – naming a way of surviving that is no longer needed. Again, it's not threatening because he'll come back with something humorous and the person feels safe and cared for. He has developed a good sense of when to push and when to shelter. "I' am a hollow tube" John says, allowing Spirit to work where it is needed.

Ann Davidson - Executive Director, retired, Powell House

John's time with me brought me creative energy and something priceless: the feeling deep in my soul that it wasn't time for me to die yet. The removal of that sword of sadness that hung over my head is the greatest blessing I could have had...

I don't know why I was attracted to John Calvi and his workshops. I just know that when I read the description in the Pendle Hill catalogue I wanted to attend. Perhaps it was the fact that he worked with victims of torture and I felt he must have acres of compassion. I was recently widowed, having been the caregiver to my husband who was an astrophysicist and high functioning on the autism spectrum. I certainly felt tortured.

That was 5 years ago and many things happened to prevent me from going, including an international move from the UK to Florida but I still felt led to see him and then this year I was diagnosed with stage 4 cancer. I wrote to him and he graciously allowed me to call and we did our first session over the phone. Just talking to him eased my mind. I didn't have any physical pain but my mental anguish was tremendous. Facing this terminal illness was huge. His words to me eased my mind and when we finished I was calmer.. more at peace and able to sort out some of my many issues.

Then in November of 2014 John came to our Meeting to present his workshop and I and my caregiver were able to attend. How wonderful to meet this cherub from heaven in person. He was/is so human and so reachable. I was fortunate to have another private session with him. And in the quiet.. with his hands held over me.. I could once again feel the Light that I, as a Quaker had been missing for sometime. This was the greatest gift I could have received.

Janny Wright – member, Saint Petersburg Friends Meeting

John Calvi has offered his workshops at Pendle Hill annually since 1990. Over the past 16 years, it has been my pleasure to welcome John to Pendle Hill, to recommend his workshops to students and friends, and to witness his amazing work as a healer and a teacher. Perhaps it was his early work as a Montessori teacher, or his massage work with tortured refugees, people with AIDS, or prisoners -- or all of the above -- but John brings a deep intuitive grace to working with people of all conditions. He meets them where they are, as they are, sensing their needs, their potential, and their limitations. Gently, firmly, and aided by a balanced blend of humor, touch, and personal stories, he encourages them to satisfy their needs, reach towards their potential, and stretch their limitations. John is a Spirit-led Friend with a deep grounding in Quaker faith and practice.

John Meyer – Communications and Outreach Coordinator, Pendle Hill

I was asked by my meeting to ask if we could interest you in coming to Saint Petersburg to give a talk, and what that would require..

Speaking for myself, for many years I have wanted to tell you about a very interesting interaction you and I had very close to twenty years ago.

You had given a talk to our Yearly Meeting, Southeastern Yearly Meeting, and after the talk you quickly approached my wife and I and said, "you need to see a Doctor there is something very wrong with your health." I did not take your advice but thru divine intervention, shortly thereafter I had a gall bladder attack and in examining that they discovered I had lung cancer.

Obviously, I had that lung and my gall bladder removed and here I am writing to you; but my wife and I still are unable to explain how you knew.

Herb Haigh – member, Saint Petersburg Friends Meeting

I was relieved to learn that almost all anthropologists and field biologists who had worked closely with an indigenous group had experienced at least one serious rift or misunderstanding with their host group due to their unintentional actions or events beyond their control. Spending less than one hour with the Quaker healer John Calvi had an even more profound affect on me. While I had not suffered as much as the torture and trauma victims John usually works with, he gently helped me accept and release some of the intense pain I had been holding from my expulsion by the Tembé. I also realized I needed to forgive myself for my actions that led to their decision and forgive the Tembé for their actions – justified or not. Finally, John helped me recognize that I had a deep calling to work with forest communities. I would be doing a great disservice to myself and the people and forests I could help in the future if I let my fear of failing stop me from trying again.

Campbell Plowden – Founder and Executive Director, Center for Amazon Community Ecology

About John Calvi

John Calvi began work as a Quaker healer when a friend needed help. He had intended to use massage to relax someone with great amounts of tension. He discovered as his hands grew hot that there was a release of energy. The friend recovered a memory of abduction and torture from many years before. John found he had a gift to release pain following trauma and it has been his study and work since that day in August 1982.

He found that trauma and pain come in many forms. Along with working in the rape crisis, in the AIDS wars, with inmates, and with tortured refugees, John has been teaching others massage and energy work for trauma. His workshops are well attended, often with a third of the class being return students wanting more.

He has also taught how one can work in crisis and avoid burnout. Healthcare professionals, hospice volunteers, family members, and mental health providers, all have occasion of witnessing too much hurt. How can we do our best for a long time and refresh along the way? All this is what John has been teaching since 1984.

After all this time, John is still learning. His gift of healing helps some people a little, some not at all, and for some there are remarkable changes, as you will read in this book.

John travels. One year towards the beginning of his work, John spoke with 35 groups around the U.S. He helped people with AIDS in several hospitals and homes in Washington, DC, as well as working in a church basement with refugees who had survived torture. Over the years this traveling work has brought him to most states, 5 prisons, 5 countries, and hospitals and homes of those with life wounds.

All along, John has lived primarily on gifts in order to serve those who cannot pay. He teaches mainly by invitation. Without the usual job security this is how it works: imagine there is some work to be done, work you are good at. Some people see this work and want it to continue so they make a gift. This leads to another invitation to do some hands-on work or teach somewhere else. John's been on the road since 1982.

John lives in a small house in the Vermont woods with his husband, Marshall Brewer. It is a sanctuary for rest and quiet that restores him.

HOW FAR HAVE YOU TRAVELED?

JOHN CALVI

How Far Have You Traveled?
True Quaker Press
Putney, Vermont
ISBN: 978-0989328524

Dedication

I dedicate this book to the memory of my dear friend, William James Kreidler. I honor him as a great teacher whose books on non-violence in the classroom have reached more than 55,000 classrooms around the world. Bill was a gifted teacher, a beloved Quaker, and a funny, fun-loving gay man. Bill would have loved the funny parts of this book. His friends and I miss him deeply since he was lost to AIDS in June of 2000. We remember his life as a bright shining of much Light that we are still happy to know and hold close. This is from Bill's keynote from the February 18, 1989, Friends for Lesbian and Gay Concerns Midwinter Gathering.

"I'm 36 years old and I finally figured out what I want to be when I grow up. I want to be an old Quaker lady. .... And before I go on I should explain what I mean by the term 'old Quaker lady'. Old Quaker ladies are the ones you see sitting in meeting. They sit with their eyes closed. (You're looking around the room.) They have a look on their faces and you can't see in the mirror but you're pretty sure that look is not on your face. It's a kind of a glow. I look at them and I think their feet are on this earth and they are hearing voices from somewhere that I am not. When I see an old Quaker lady in meeting I'm never sure what the right word to use is - if it's serenity or ecstasy. Maybe they're not mutually exclusive. Now, an old Quaker lady isn't necessarily old, isn't necessarily a woman, and isn't necessarily a Quaker. In fact, one of the best descriptions I've ever come across is one that Victor Hugo wrote in *Les Misérables* and he is describing, in fact, an old Catholic woman. He says, "her life, which had been a series of pious works, had cloaked her in a kind of transparent whiteness, and in growing old she had acquired the beauty of goodness, what had been thinness in her youth, was in her maturity a transparency, and through this transparency the angel could be seen." Now Friends, I read that and thought, "Hot damn—that's for me!"

Introduction

I've been watching people in the places I work. I watch very carefully to see something in particular. Who is serving long term in a crisis and not becoming a victim of burnout? How is it that one can witness ongoing pain and suffering and continue to offer their best? How does that work?

The core of this book is about goodness and knowing your goodness. I am suggesting that knowing your goodness offers strength and balance for hard work, specifically the hard work of healing one's self and others. While my first book, *The Dance Between Hope & Fear*, speaks to healing trauma, this second book describes an underlying dynamic that makes the path smoother.

So there is it. I've seen something I want to show you. It's about goodness and knowing it yourself. Seeking how things become is great work. I hope this will be part of your seeking.

John Calvi

PO Box 301

Putney VT 05346

Acknowledgments

I've had three courageous editors in getting this book to print. Shelly Angel has read my entire collection of writing. Just as she did with my first book, she chose the content and shaped this book in its current form. Her understanding of this work and capacity to reveal it in writing is unsurpassed. Maia Simon wrangled the manuscript into unity, readability, and clearest meaning – a talent of mind and fortitude I could not have done without. Excellent work that's done as a gift is extreme generosity- such gifts mean making books and living simply is possible. These editors have gone beyond all best hopes to do more and did so very well. Marshall Brewer has read and reread everything I've ever written fearlessly, without wincing, and with a giant eraser at the ready. Nothing grand in my life happens without his good presence and gracefulness.

Heather Taylor of Blue Heron Images and Words made a gift of the charts at the center of the book. She is talented in the many ways of communication and a good friend and neighbor.

John Meyer's author photo on the cover is another gift of excellence in the work of making this book. His portraits of both Marshall and me are the best photos we have.

The quote by William James Kreidler is used by permission of his estate, Charles McCorkle, executor, for which I am very grateful.

I want to thank *Friends Journal* for their faithful service to the Religious Society of Friends, Quakers. Their good work of providing ideas, news, and information about Friends for so many years is a large and important work that I and many others are very grateful for. They were the first to publish my writing, brave souls and editors that they are.

The core of this book is recent writing and is based on teaching the goodness workshops since 2001. The rest of this book has been written over many years and in many places. I want to acknowledge some of the many places where I've sought quiet hours alone sitting at a table by the window writing-

The homes of friends in so many places, impossible to name them all - Teru Simon in Vermont, Rosa Packard in Connecticut, Elizabeth Watson in Minnesota, John Meyer in Washington, DC, Liz Keeney in Ohio, Chuck Bauer in Wisconsin, JoAnn Brewer in California, Mark Scheuer in

Tennessee, Cecilia George in Texas, Nancy Pocock in Ontario, Lyle Jenks in Pennsylvania, Glenn White in Oregon, Mary Ann Downey in Georgia, Dennis Barrett in Colorado, and many more.

The guest quarters of Quaker meetings have been key to my writing retreats: Santa Fe Friends Meeting in New Mexico, Pima Friends Meeting in Arizona, Orlando Friends Meeting in Florida, Toronto Friends Meeting in Ontario, University Friends Meeting in Seattle, and more. And the Quaker conference centers: Pendle Hill in Pennsylvania, Quaker Center in California, and both Quaker Hill and Earlham College in Indiana.

Putney Friends Meeting in Vermont is where I began my work within a spiritual community. I was a Released Friend under the care of this meeting from 1987 to 2000. My membership with Quakers is there, along with a long history of caring for people in need and receiving support. New England Yearling Meeting has also made good use of me over the years and has also provided support. A good springboard into the world is a great help in the quest to be well used.

How Far Have you Traveled?

CONTENTS

Section 1

How Far Have You Traveled?

Plenary for Midwinter Gathering

Friends for Lesbian and Gay Concerns

February 14, 2003,

Ghost Ranch, Abiquiú, New Mexico

Dear Great and Holy Spirit,
Be with me now as I do this work.
Guide me with your wisdom.
Help me to be a vessel of your love
that we may each receive comfort, healing, and protection.

It is a lovely honor for me to be invited to speak with you tonight. This is a nomadic community that I have traveled with for 24 years. That's a long time to be with a village, especially a village that keeps moving.

You might remember a talk we had some time ago by our good friend, Bill Kreidler, who was one of our most wonderful Quaker teachers. I dedicate this talk to him tonight. I want to talk about spiritual life, something he thought was very important, that we should all share with one another to help us keep current about what we're noticing on the inside.

There's a traditional greeting in Tibet: "How far have you traveled?" It's a broad, open question. It leaves space to share how difficult the road has been. Maybe it asks what you have seen. Maybe it suggests that you might know something I might need to know if I'm going in that direction. In some ways such a question opens the possibility of saying how much it hurts to be on the road, how difficult the journey is. It asks for some sharing and sometimes it results in information that maybe we don't even know yet that we need.

I want to talk with you tonight about how far I have traveled, especially in the time I have known this organization, this collection of peculiar people. I first came to Friends for Lesbian and Gay Concerns in 1979.

If you're like me and you try to learn from your mistakes, sometimes you get the feeling that there are no holidays or summer vacations in this school. I am able to look back on a lot of mistakes and see that there are things I've learned along the way, some things I want to keep track of.

As we go on our spiritual journey, as we are traveling to places where there are a lot of unknowns - maybe we're traveling on the inside and maybe we're traveling out in the world - I think one thing is very important. There will always be something called unexpected help. There will be some help that comes along that we don't ask for, maybe that we don't even know we need or want. Maybe it doesn't come right at the moment when we think it should happen. It's hard to schedule divine intervention, of course. But unexpected help has a lovely and surprising way of showing up.

When I was seventeen years old, I realized that being gay was not going to be a phase. I realized that I was a lifer and I was going to grow to be a big old queen no matter what I did. Unfortunately there was no one around then to tell me how much fun it was going to be! It scared me so much that I wrote a few notes and climbed up onto the roof of my parents' house. I sat above the second story, over a slab of concrete, and took out my brother's Colt .45 revolver, which he brought home from the American war in Viet Nam, and I attempted suicide. I pulled the trigger. My hand was shaking so much that I fired just above my head, and a little angelic voice in the back of my mind said, "Well, this isn't going to work."

It was a lovely intervention and I learned that the voice wasn't speaking just for that moment. In the days and months following, that voice said, "Oh, well, let's figure something else out here. We'll keep going, get on down the road. Maybe it won't be as bad as we think. Maybe there'll be some good things along the way."

About fifteen years later the AIDS epidemic began. I had left my job as a preschool teacher. I had spent ten years working with young children and we had a good time together. But I decided I needed to do different work, so I went to massage school and while I was there began specializing in massage for trauma. With AIDS, a huge opportunity to do compassionate work came along. I was at the beginning of the work and still figuring out how massage could be used to make a beautiful gift to someone who is frightened, to someone who had lost hope, to someone who was in a great deal of pain, and to someone who was leaving life so quickly he didn't know how to gather any grace around his situation.

When I was almost 30 years old, I was thrown out of my family for being gay. Now, it wasn't such a bad family to get thrown out of, but I won't go into that. It was a difficult thing and I had a great deal of sadness and depression. I got a lot of massage and psychotherapy, and as the depression began to lift, I wrote a song. It was a beautiful song, a wonderful song. As I composed that song, the depression lifted entirely. I knew that coming out was very important work and I knew that it was spiritual work. I sent the song backstage to one of my favorite singers, Meg Christian. And lo and behold, she recorded that song at Carnegie Hall. I was just starting my AIDS work when she recorded it. So, suddenly, I had sufficient royalties from that song to buy a good professional massage table to go into the AIDS epidemic and do lots of good work. I had been asking for help along the way but still this came as a great surprise.

One day when I was working on a fellow, I found myself very afraid. Right in the midst of my fear, lovely spirits were coming into the room saying, "John, John, John—get a grip, honey! You are not doing this alone. You're not doing any of this alone. As a matter of fact, you never work alone. We are always with you. We will always guide you. Whenever the work is beautiful, it will be because we are helping you to make it beautiful."

Only a few other people were doing massage that early in the epidemic. It was very scary because we didn't know it was a virus. I was trying to be graceful, but was afraid that I was going to get sick too. I was afraid that this fellow was going to die before we could reach a moment of beautiful compassion. Here again was this stunning unexpected help, help that I didn't even know to call for, help that was hard for me to surrender to. But it stripped my gears, and I did surrender.

When I began doing massage most of the people on my table were women who had been sexually assaulted; most of them didn't have any money to pay for massage. I wrote a letter to a hundred people and said, "I am doing something beautiful, will you help me?" Half of them wrote back and said, "I'll help you." A lot of people at this conference did. From that time I was able to do compassionate work by living on gifts, asking people to help me go out and make a gift, a spiritual gift.

Asking is something that has slowly, slowly, become graceful within me. And when the help comes, it's always a wondrous surprise and always a delight. Even though it's not unexpected and I have done the asking, it's lovely to find out help is available. Then I must do the work of receiving, which might even be harder than asking.

Another large task for me has been gathering patience and mercy for myself. This has been difficult, ongoing work. There are parts of myself that I'm not quite sure what to do with, such as old anger and fear. Maybe I don't like how they work or how they look. I need to learn how to be patient and merciful with myself so I can share that with other people. Sometimes I'll find myself in a situation and make mistakes or trip up; I must find some way to be graceful with the work and toward myself and not berate myself.

Back in 1985 I was among the first team of people to go into New York state prisons to offer AIDS education to employees and inmates. We went in to this one prison up near the Canadian border, a big, old, scary thing. I was terrified. I hadn't worked in prisons before. It was unnerving for me.

After a tour, we were sitting in a room full of prisoners for a time. I could feel the inmates were getting restless, and I wanted to get started. I turned to the warden and asked if we could start; he said, "No, we're waiting for one more fellow." So, as we sat there waiting, down the hall comes the sound of chains clanking and into the room comes this huge man, all bound up in chains and leather restraints with guards around him. They escort him to the back of the room and take half the chains off. I immediately thought, "Oh, my God, this is so inhuman, this is so awful that this should ever happen to anyone." That was my first response.

My second response was, "We're in a maximum-security prison. He's a really big guy. I'm in a group of murderers. He probably has big problems with anger. He gets angry, you die." I had this feeling that maybe it's appropriate that he is some distance from me and in restraints.

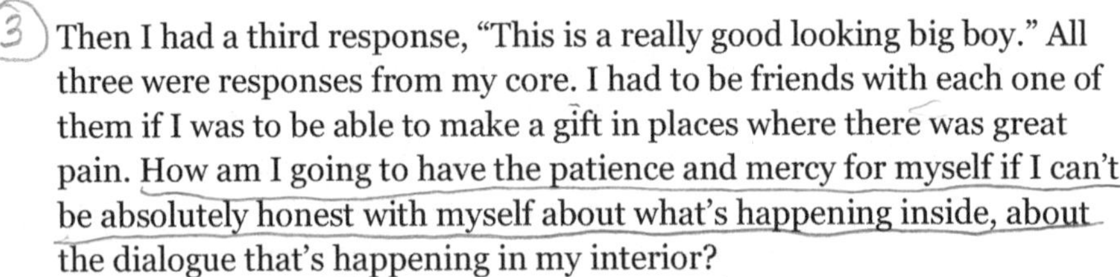

Then I had a third response, "This is a really good looking big boy." All three were responses from my core. I had to be friends with each one of them if I was to be able to make a gift in places where there was great pain. How am I going to have the patience and mercy for myself if I can't be absolutely honest with myself about what's happening inside, about the dialogue that's happening in my interior?

There was another time that was even a little bit more embarrassing though it was a little bit less external. I had been invited to teach at several yearly meetings; at one point I was invited to do an AIDS education session for Young Friends. I went in and taught "AIDS 101" for a bunch of teenagers. There was a wonderful college freshman - a handsome, good looking boy - who took me aside and said, "Mr. Calvi, I need to talk with you about something personal and private", and I said, "Okay." "Mr. Calvi, I can't find any condoms that are large enough." Do you know that feeling you get when the Universe is playing coyote with you and it's just sort of saying, "Yeah, you think you've got grace? Deal with this, fool. Deal with this."

I found his problem a rather large distraction, but I was able to come up with a reasonable response and not scream or blush or leave the room.

But it's absolutely vital that I know for me that there are all kinds of distractions to doing sacred work. I have to embrace those aspects of me that are the detours and not be surprised and not be shocked; I can make friends with them and not let them become obstacles. Making friends with the distraction is to lighten the burden, to have more honesty and more Light within myself.

Another obstacle for me is fear. I grew up surrounded by a great deal of violence and alcoholism, so my capacity to become frightened is quite large. Sometimes, I have been called into situations where my fear will interrupt the work I intend to do. I am always looking for ways to work, to be in the Light, and not be overwhelmed by the fear of my own healing journey or what I witness in others' lives.

I was teaching massage to a dozen murdering rapists in prison; this was in the midst of doing my own rape/incest work from childhood. It was a very hard day's work. Over in the corner of the chapel one fellow was doing some massage work I had taught and I saw that he was going in the wrong direction. I went over to say, "If you go down the arm instead of up, it will feel better at his shoulder." As I approached him he turned to me and said, "You know, I don't even remember killing my wife. The prison psychologist says I may never remember. It must have been me, because I was the only one there and we were doing lots of drugs. We used to do massage; she gave a great massage."

On the outside I was saying, "Hmm"; on the inside I was saying, "How did I get in here? Whose work is this?" So I created a mantra for myself; "John, this is mere terror. It's just terror. Just let it move through."

There was another time that was even scarier for me, scarier because of my ignorance. Often when I am at a large Quaker gathering I hang around at the edges so people can come and have private conversations with me. I was at a yearly meeting sitting on the edge of a big crowd having a picnic. A woman came over to me and we were talking alone together and she said, "You're like Jesus aren't you?" and I thought, "Uh-oh, this is going to be good, whatever this is, it's going to be large." And I said, "No, I'm not so much like Jesus as I am like Howdy Doody, frankly, but we can talk about whatever you like." She terrified me when she began to tell me that she had both a penis and a vagina. She began to tell me her life story. I became terrified because I was afraid that she was going to ask something of me and I had no ideas about this topic. I knew nothing. I became a complete coward. As I listened to her story and sat there calmly on the outside, a part of me on the inside said, "John, just listen to what's being said. What is the essence of this? What's the essence of what she's expressing?" That essence was loneliness. Who could she confide in? Who could she talk to? Could she actually talk to someone like me and not have me run away scared and screaming? It had always been a gamble for her this entire life. We talked long enough for me to stop being afraid. We talked long enough so we understood one another and we weren't strangers anymore. It's a hard thing to do with terror. Mostly, it has to do with not wanting to be uncomfortable in large ways. Mostly, this fear has to do with what we don't know.

~ ~ ~ ~

As someone who came up through schools before learning disabilities were invented, and being very learning disabled, I ran into lots of bumps, especially in high school. One of the things that became clear to me as I got out into the world was that I really didn't want fame. What I really wanted more than anything was to be really good at something.

A lot of Quakerism is like that. It's as if you were walking in the woods or on a beach, and you found a stone. Somehow you knew that stone was there for you to pick up and carry home with you. You wanted everyone to see how rare and significant that stone was, so you started polishing it, not to show off the stone but to bring out its beauty and worth so others could see it, too. Similarly, you find an aspect of Quakerism that feels important to you, something you feel passionate about. You settle into it and polish it, like the stone. You come to know it and use it and work with it. You are healing your own life and helping other people with their lives by the Light that shines from the stone you polish.

I used to write a lot of songs. I performed music and once upon a time I got an invitation to do a benefit concert. I was performing with Pete Seeger. We were just about to walk on stage for the second half, and I was standing right behind him. He's one of the very few heroes in my life; I was trying to think of something to say to him that wouldn't sound stupid. I wanted to honor him without sounding like just another fan. I was just about to say something when he turned to me and he said, "Your songs are really good." "Thank you," I said, "thank you."

Some years back, I realized I had settled into a groove and had gotten good at something. I could see it and feel it and someone else could see it and feel it. Miles Frieden asked me to speak at a gay and lesbian statewide gathering in Maine. I got there a little bit early and was sitting in the bleachers waiting for another speaker on the program. The gymnasium began to fill up. Sitting in front of me was a large woman, a big girl, a very big woman. We're talking tall, wide, round; she had a deep voice and was saying to her friend next to her that she had hurt her back lifting an engine out of a car. Yes, this was a big girl. And when she sat down in front of me, my hands began to heat up. I had a very clear message that the pain was down in her lower left back and if I would be permitted to touch her, I could release that pain. I got that message in the same way we get a message in meeting for worship.

Now, I'm sitting there behind her and I'm trying to think of how I'm going to do this. How am I going to get my hands on her? I saw the headlines flashing before my eyes: "Amazon tears Quaker in twain!" But I found a moment in the conversation when she was talking about her pain, how it had been going on for a couple of weeks, and I leaned over one shoulder and said, "And it's in your lower left back, right?" She said, "Yes." And I said, "I think if you put both feet flat on the floor and if you take a deep breath, I'm just going to do some gentle touches back here. I think I can move this out." And we did just a little work with her deep breathing and I did some gentle touches. And she turned around to me and she said, "This is a spiritual gift?" And I said, "Yes." And she said, "You do this with your church?" I said, "Yes." She said, "That's pretty good."

It's good to polish a stone and find a way to be of use so the Light that you're working with isn't about you. It's about the Light that you can pass on, the Light that you can share while keeping the Light on the road setting a tone so that Light gets passed. There's a lot in our culture that works against this. It's very important-- especially being Friends in this time when there is such warmongering -- that we polish that stone and shine that Light in all the individual ways that we have.

One of the largest difficulties for me in my journey, in my spiritual seeking, has been surrender, surrender to Light, surrender to true love. But I have found that there are occasions when these qualities can cross paths and inform one another. If you can learn some surrender in the category of surrendering to the Light, you might be able to transfer that wisdom to surrendering to true love. Or you might be able to do it the other way round. They are both about trust and intimacy. When my lovely husband Marshall and I first met, he said to me, "Teach me something about massage." I didn't want to tell him what I did right after we first met; I thought there was no sense scaring him on the third date. So I said. "OK, I'll teach you something about massage. You feel this lump in my back? It's a place where the muscles get very tense and tight and they all bunch together. Put your hands flat on that place and take a deep breath, a long, slow, deep breath, and as you let that breath go, think about how much you love me." That knot in my back disappeared just like that and his eyes popped open, and I said, "That's something about massage."

Surrender is an important work in the spiritual journey. There are lots of reasons to be afraid of it. There are lots of reasons to deny it and to postpone it and to set it aside. It gets confused with giving up. It gets confused with giving over power. But I would ask you, in your own spiritual journey, to keep track of those places in your own life where you have experienced surrender and what it came to teach you. Where is the next opportunity coming from?

Sometimes the work that is coming to us is so subtle that it's hard to hear. The spiritual guidance that's coming to us - - opportunities that are opening, that we're being called to, the gifts that we have to share - these can be easily missed in our noisy culture. Sometimes they are so subtle that we don't hear them the first time around. It might be that something very large has to come around to better catch our attention. Sometimes it's a visitation, but we live in a culture that doesn't talk about spiritual life very much. American popular culture is so loud and so noisy. There are a lot of subtle, quiet things we don't hear. It's important to listen very carefully and quietly, and as well as possible, and to look for that guidance.

Once upon a time I was working with a lovely woman from El Salvador who had been tortured by the treasury police in many different ways, ways that I won't even describe. It was so frightening to be a witness to that pain that sometimes I would find myself shaking, afraid that I would actually feel the pain that she had felt in her body. Feeling another's pain is not uncommon in my experience of healing work. One day when she was ready to release some of the largest pain, Jesus came into the room. Now, I'd heard about him for a long time and I figured he was a good fellow, but it's not like we had been introduced; I was very surprised. The work that happened then, the extent of the work that took place, the release was stunning.

A few years later I was working with a group of Cambodian

grandmothers, all of whom had been tortured by the Khmer Rouge. We were working in the house of a Buddhist priest. I was working with one lovely grandmother - - I think she was the oldest, she may have seen the most - - and who comes into the room but the Buddha. Stunning. Very different from Jesus, very different - and who am I to argue with who shows up? It was so lovely and so graceful. The tone and the feeling were very, very different, but the release of her pain was absolutely beautiful in the same way.

A couple of years ago, I was invited to do AIDS work in Mexico. A friend took us to an ancient religious site called Monte Albán and said, "Sit over here on this rock, it's an energy source of the old religions." So, Marshall and I sat on the stone and, of course, went into Quaker worship. While we were in the quiet, I had a vision, a visitation of lovely elders dressed in blue and red robes, and they came and they said, "Welcome, welcome. We are so glad you are witnessing this place in a manner of reverence, and we want you to know that we held the reverence here long before you came. We were the reverence here before your religion in your times, and your frame of reference about the universe is actually a little small for us." This was so subtle and quiet. If this had happened to me when I first came to Quakerism, I wouldn't have seen it. But after 35 years of being a Quaker, I could hear the quiet enough to feel that subtlety, to let it come through.

There are still difficult parts of myself I work with and struggle to understand, things that are painful for me, where I can't quite see the handles, and I don't know how they work. I was beaten and raped as a young child, and some years ago the rape nightmares increased. They were so fierce and relentless that I settled into a rut of anger. It was fierce, and it was large, and it came to be that the anger was the largest and most available emotion to me. It was ferocious. It would wake me up in the middle of the night and it wouldn't let me get back to sleep. The anger would attach to anything that I thought of and I became furious. It was powerful and frightening. The only relief that I had was to work, to go into situations where there was a great deal of pain, say my prayers for disciplines of grace, surrender to the Light, and to do the touching work. At those times the anger would be set aside, and that was a great comfort to me.

There was a small number of friends who misdiagnosed me as having spiritual arrogance and withdrew their friendship. This was very difficult, but what was even more difficult was how intensely my heart would close, that I would become so illogically furious that I could not receive care. I got a lot of help with this condition and began to learn how it was organized within me. I began to understand some of the new needs and new cycles I had come to in my own healing. I am still learning about forgiveness, about holding the beauty of life and the pain of life in the same glance without wincing, without getting stuck in the pain, without trying to be romantically in love with the beauty of the world. I am learning to hold them both equally in front of me. It's a hard task, and I think probably one that I will be working on for the rest of my life.

~ ~ ~ ~

I want to talk about an idea I'm working with: that Quakerism is a little bit like true love. If you find true love, and decide you're going to stay with that person and you're going to do marriage or something like marriage, you'll probably be surprised to find out that you could be seven years into it, and you are still at the beginning, still unpacking because it's large work. There are subtle pieces to it. There are large pieces to it. There's a lot of unpacking to do. Quakerism is the same way. Now that I have been a Quaker for almost four decades, I feel like I am just now getting down to pay dirt. There are such subtleties. One of the things I like to do as I travel and teach at other meetings is to watch some of the old Quakers.

You might remember back in the beginning when you first came to Quakers, you began trying it on to see if the shoe would fit. You may remember that it was a fairly romantic experience with this ooh-la-la feeling to it. It was exciting. It was romantic, large, and lush. But if you look at some of the old girls and some of the old boys who have been Quakers for a long time, they do what I call schlepping the Light. It is not a large, dramatic thing that they do, and I'm not saying that they do it more easily or more consistently. What has happened is that they integrated Quaker principles into their lives so that it's a natural movement that they are able to do over and over as they respond to everyday life with reverence. As Bill Kreidler told us back in his 1989 talk, he wanted to grow up to be an old Quaker lady. I would like to live long enough and study long enough to become someone who schleps the Light. Not to be a big showy thing, but an engaging, natural thing that I could do in a continuous way. That would be lovely.

I want to close with a little bit about FLGC: it is this wonderful, nomadic group that throws a big party and then folds the tents and goes away to a lot of different places, and then comes back again. Over the years we have done lots of talking about who we are and how it is that we come together. There are times when we talk about ourselves being a force, both spiritual and political, and there are other times when we talk about ourselves being an oasis; I have thought of us in those terms. However, my current understanding is this: by coming together in our delight, in our celebration, and in our grief, we are actually battery rechargers for one another. By coming together we do not make a large political force here; that's not what happens. But every person here, when he or she goes back home, living a normal life, takes a charge from this gathering, takes a bolt of light and goes home and continues seeking in our manner. And, of course, in Quakerism the spiritual life and the political life are melded and integrated and constantly worked and constantly unfolding. It's an ongoing masterpiece.

What we strive for here is to make an open village where there is room for everyone. There is not room for every behavior, however. There are certain cultural behaviors we want to embody such as tenderness, respect, dignity, a capacity to listen, and a capacity to speak as clearly as we are able. We do this to make a good village life so that everyone has the opportunity to grow and change and expand into our best selves. We come together and create a village, which is a nearly impossible task. We charge up and then we disperse. We become the queer Quaker diaspora. And we go out, and make some good Godly trouble, and do our lives in large ways. We fall out of love, we fall in love, we make families, we take on outrageous work, and then we come back and gather into the circle and tell each other how far have we traveled.

~ ~ ~ ~

Q - In the process of channeling someone else's pain, how do you let it out so it doesn't stay in?

JC – This a wonderful study and has mostly to do with understanding that no matter how much training you have, no matter how much skill or talent, your entire spiritual goal is to be a good cardboard tube. Any energy that comes into you from above is a gift for the receiver and any exchange of energy that comes out is not initiated by you. I am only a cardboard tube and my task is to be a good one.

There are several things along these lines that are not only good for doing energy work in helping people to heal from trauma, but they are also a very good discipline for witness that involves observing others' pain. For instance, if you're doing social change work and see a great deal of pain, here are some things to keep track of.

You want to know about the pain of your life. Each of us has pain. You want to be fluent with it. You want to know about the parts that you understand and the homework you have gotten done. And you want to have an updated list of those things you do not understand, the things that still need work. If you understand the nature of pain in your own life, you can keep it separate from other people's pain and avoid confusion.

There's also the task of loving your life. No matter what you witness, you want to understand that life may be hard but it is also beautiful. You want to love your life. You want to have things around you that make you glad to be here, that make you juicy. You want to increase those things. You want to know what things bring you to your best and honor you. You want to have more of them. At the same time, you want to take those things that do not bring you to your best, do not honor you, and set them aside.

Another thing to understand is that pain has function. All conflict and trouble have function, which is essentially sacred learning. Without trouble, no one would show up to learn anything. I wouldn't. I'd say, "Summer vacation all year? I'm in!" But because there is trouble, because there is pain, there are things we need to do and things we need learn.

At some point, all of us are going to witness someone else's pain and find it is too difficult for us to work with. Then we have to say no. Other times there's going to be pain we can work with. By following these disciplines, the range of what we can work with is going to increase. Our capacity to carry Light is going to increase.

Q – How can we raise our children so they will not learn this culture's hatred of gay people?

JC – Everyone has gay relatives or friends. Have we made them welcome? Have we brought them in? Do we understand that this is a difference, a flavor we can put into the soup? Do we bring it to the soup because it has that flavor? Do we honor it? Do our children see that we honor it?

Q – How can we respond when we are asked to do things beyond our gifts, or knowledge, or comfort?

JC – We have done a lot of spiritual homework and we're no longer volunteering for work that is inappropriate to our skill package. We know what we're good at and we're doing it. The problem is there's too much to do. Why is there too much to do? We have got both serious greed and serious suffering on the planet.

The first thing is that we do not do good works to save the world. We do good works to come closer to the Divine, to reform our interiors, to find the Light within us that is our God-given gift to the world.

Our task actually is to clean that Light and make it bright. It is our task to do our best. It is not our task to do our most. Your best is fabulous. My best is fabulous. What do I need to do my best for a long time?

We need a certain about of work. It's always going to be less than what's needed. You can look in any corner of the world and see a hundred things that need doing. Out of that hundred you might actually have talent and expertise for ten. Out of the ten you might have time for doing two. If those two fit you -- if you make friends with them and make a commitment -- then you can do that work for a long time. The planet does not need for us to do good works for a short time, but to do them for a long time.

Q – Is it necessary to identify yourself as a Quaker healer?

JC – I get invited to work in many different kinds of situations. There are times when I'm working when there is no opportunity to identify. I might be at a bus stop and sit next to someone and my hands get hot. I've got an angel whispering in one ear saying, "The person sitting next to you lost her mom at seven years old and now that pain is in her low back. You could move that out. I will work through you." My response is, "Thank you for another opportunity to love." It might be that people hear something in my voice. If they do, they might understand that I can be of help.

Sometimes I have to do some theater to connect me with that person. In other words, sometimes the identification as a Quaker healer is not necessary. There are times when the identification might be harmful and so I don't try to explain what I'm doing. Doing so might actually interrupt the work.

I use whatever identity makes it easiest to be heard. There are some churches, for instance, where I don't talk about being gay until I'm close to the door at the end of my talk. I want them to hear what I have to say first and have them think there's the possibility that I am with them as a child of God before their understanding is disrupted with news of something else.

One of the first things that Quakers got thrown in jail for was to say they did miracles. It freaked a lot of people out. So the healing that Quakers did became secret. George Fox caught a lot of trouble for doing healing work, but he wasn't very good about shutting up about it. There were a number of Friends saying, "George, you are going to get yourself up on a pedestal and you're going to make trouble for Friends. Stop it." And so his Book of Miracles was destroyed. It was later reconstituted by someone who spent an awful lot of time in the library. It's something to be careful with. Are we using an identifier to build a bridge or is it being used out of ego?

Q – Unprogrammed Friends seem to condescend to other Quakers.

JC – I was at a Quaker retreat a while ago and we played a game where you changed seats if your group was named. Someone called out, "Everyone with a PhD!" Half of the people changed seats. Conversely, I have the honor of being a high school graduate.

There is a difficulty among Friends of being in a class from which we have to build bridges to people who are not in that class. We often don't do it well. One of the good things is that most Quakers didn't start out here.

I am first generation, working class Italian-American. When I went to my first Quaker meeting at Wesleyan University, I changed the average education level and the class balance there. There's a lot of that going on.

There is a concern that we don't know how to reach other classes and people of color. There's no problem in being educated, but are there things about our lives that are keeping us from reaching others with whom we want to engage? This is a vigil we have to keep.

Section 2

Light Schlepped and Washed

Georgina's Morning

May 1996

setting down the phone and settling into prayer
reaching with all my heart for the hurt one
in a moment of calm and care
I feel this one who I love
and know her pain

going outside
scooping wet earth into a dish
push the white candles into the earth
light each one as it sits on my desk
a prayer for the hurt one
all my heart for her

grateful for the pure moment
honored by the trust
and by the need
reaching to the one
who will be well
later when more work is worked
when more seeing
and feeling
and burning
and melting
is worked

reaching
reaching
hoping to get through
with this gift of love

Preparations

October 1997

She moved through the ancient hemlock trees like one of them - ponderous, swaying side to side. She stepped with the reverence of walking among holy elders. Her thoughts, too, moved slowly, as though pushed by a breeze, one to the next. First, she wondered why the power of old women couldn't be more external and more easily seen. Why did it have to be so internal and subtle? Why did the young have to wait until they tangle with the old to see the strength of age? Her thoughts came back again to the trees, so old, so full of wood and air, so full of their own being, and so patient with everything else - time, weather, light, and this small old woman. Walking on centuries of fallen needles with the feeling of being in a great cathedral, and of walking through an old friend, she wondered what she would witness this night.

With each step she rested her body, spread her toes, and walked a bit more slowly to gather in the gracious good rhythm of the trees. She felt herself sink a bit more into her legs. A quiet walk through here, now, as the light of day began to ebb, was perfect preparation. She was glad not to have come through town and to have seen no one on her arrival. After soaking in the surroundings as though embraced by family, and feeling the softening of her body, she turned all her senses toward reverence and seeking. Decades of this practice had taught her that the Divine was always near, and she was never alone. Contact was always hers to make and it was never anything less than thrilling.

Soon, the clearing with the meetinghouse came into view. Old and dignified, it sat alone, far away from town and all the movement and noise that people impose. She stood still and beheld it as though she were a child seeing a beloved mother. Her heart gave thanks and she set about making it ready. She opened every door and window. She swept the porch and the main room. She gathered chairs and benches into a large horseshoe shape, saving a favorite for herself at the head, facing the door. With all this movement, music rose in her; not songs so much as phrases, old hymns, chants, something to repeat and grow in resonance. Her hands became warmer. What had seemed daunting work earlier in the day now became a task she was eager for.

Soon it was time to light candles and close most of the windows. She set a light on the porch to guide people up the steps and returned to her chair. She sat, full of expectancy, knowing she would be guided. As she said her prayers, the memories and visions of other nights here in this meetinghouse came, unasked. How many years had she been doing Meeting for Healing? How many heads had she cradled as tears rolled down cheeks, surrendering pain and despair? What became of the young man with the crooked smile? And that woman who seemed to change only on the inside? Was that here or somewhere else? The years, faces, and stories wove a life she could no longer recall in sequence.

She had some fear, of course. There was pain that scared her and made her weary, that might lead to days of recovery when she did not make sense even to herself. But her fear had always been embraced by knowing that she never worked alone. Her friends in high places were good friends and the places were very high. She wondered if there would be lessons for her tonight. Sometimes it was easy, with work that was clear and straightforward. Sometimes there was a pattern or energy that captured her attention and made her more and more curious until she could see its essence and understand its contours.

There she sat, hands pulsing, eyes on the path, thoughts floating above the candlelight as she heard the first people arriving.

The Largest Group

Peacework - March 1998 American Friends Service Committee, New England

I am sitting in a therapist's waiting room. She is not my therapist and I am not waiting for an appointment with her. I am here because a new client had called her and asked for a late appointment, a time when no one else would be in the office building. This stranger's voice gave her a gut level feeling of possible danger; might he hurt her in an explosion of rage, especially if they were obviously alone? She thought it best to have someone visibly on hand tonight to deter any potential for violence. She is not a small woman nor is she without power. Last winter when she heard deer hunters shooting on her posted land, she strapped on her boots, flew down through the woods, and gave those trespassers some holy Quaker hell that they would not soon forget.

So I've come here to sit in her waiting room, be a presence, and to write about something that's been on my mind this past year. There are many groups of people in pain. The world is full of various groups of hurting people. I've made some study of this. I have taught massage in prisons, given energy work to tortured refugees, and taught spiritual disciplines to heroin addicts with AIDS.

But here's what I've been thinking about: The largest group of hurt people on the planet are women with sexual hurt - women demeaned by sexual harassment, women sexually abused in childhood, women sexually assaulted. In every group of people from every continent, this burden of sexual hurt is frequently an additional part of women's history. Perhaps it is so commonplace throughout human time that we do not see it as clearly apart and distinct from plague, famine, escape from war, or war itself.

The sense that this common thread weaves women's lives together around the globe is almost too much to take in. Yet, as I connect the dots of what I have seen and heard, I know that it is so, and I grieve. The reality of sexual hurt is a horrible burden. As someone who has survived rape as a young child, I know too well the nature of the pain and the tremendous work that its healing entails. The list of damages is long and ugly: diminished self-worth, physical illness, trust broken nearly beyond repair, and flaming swirls of anger, fear, guilt, and sadness. I wonder if truly safe places are few and far between, where and when can healing begin?

What are we doing about this? What are we doing about this as individuals? What are we doing about this through our Meetings? What are we doing about this with our votes and our money? Are we bringing it into our prayers and into our planning about what the world needs? Does it give us any ideas for focus for our volunteer or professional work? Do we share our deep feelings about this to help the wounded know they are not alone on a silent mountain climb? The largest group of hurt people in the world is women with sexual hurt. And we are doing . . . what?

Schlepping the Light

Intermountain Yearly Meeting, Keynote Address
Ghost Ranch, Abiquiú, New Mexico
June 9, 2004

Dear Great and Holy Spirit, be with me now as I do this work. Help me to be a vessel of your love that we all may receive comfort, healing, and protection.

Friends, I am honored to be with you this week. It is a blessing for me to be back at Ghost Ranch with you. I am very grateful to the elders who are sitting and holding me in the Light as I speak with you today. Dennis Barrett, Bev McCauley, Pelican Lee, and Rebecca Henderson have been holding me in the Light and keeping me in prayer, and I feel very ready to speak with you.

I am not a scholar. I am not a learned, weighty Friend. I am, in short, nothing fancy. But I do lots of traveling among Friends and I began to notice that there are Friends that you can sit next to in Meeting for Worship and feel them go into prayer. You can feel their centering. You can feel their deep faith and their capacity to generate Light begin to change them, the people around them, and the room that they're in.

A couple of years ago I began to talk with old Friends - of course, "old" is a dangerous word, isn't it? "Old" seems to be about fifteen years older than yourself, at least. After talking with several Friends older than I am, I began to pose the question: how do Friends bring their spiritual life deeper, so it isn't just skin level, it's not just intellectual? How is it that someone can reflect their connection with the Divine in Meeting for Worship, in their communication with the Divine, with their breath, their walk, and the way they respond to everyday living situations?

I am not talking about weighty Friends; the kind you hope might accept the job of clerk of your Meeting. I am talking about people who are power generators of the Light. I am talking about people whose spiritual life is so deep that you can feel it when they say, "Good morning." I am not talking about heroes or saints, but very plain people. It might be that their house is a mess. It might be that when you think of them you think, "Remember the apple tart that she made? My God, it was dog's lunch, wasn't it?" I am talking about those Friends who carry and work with and live in the Light most of the time, in ways that can be felt.

Now schlepping is a wonderful old word; it means to drag. It means unceremonious. It means no drama, no romance, it means everyday and common. I'm seeking to understand the Friends who have the most grace with the least effort and the least fanfare, those who schlep the Light.

I once saw this very clearly. I was in a room where a young man began to weep, and an old Quaker woman just scooped him up and held him and rocked him until he was finished weeping. She then went back to prayer. It was a simple, beautiful act. It was especially beautiful because this happened in prison. I was teaching energy work and as I was working on this young man, he suddenly became aware of what had happened in his life and what the consequences were. He had murdered someone to impress his girl friend. He was 20 years old and had been convicted to 25 years in prison. As soon as he got to prison he got a letter from this girlfriend that said, "Oh, never mind." It took him a while to really understand all the implications. He was embarrassed to be weeping in front of all the other prisoners. What he needed was a hug and a kiss and then some detachment. It took a great deal of Light to let him go after he was finished weeping.

I spoke mostly to Friends who were in their 80s. One was a young 55. Two were in their 90s. One was 96, and talked about taking a horse and buggy to a wedding at someone's house in Iowa where the Quaker ladies all wore hats and the men were in dark clothes. This gave me a sense of a much longer perspective.

I really am talking about a rare condition; it's not something each of us should be aspiring to; we each have different gifts. It is important to take notice of those people who sink deeply into the Spirit in a way that others can feel. It is important to be mindful of this, because these people are generators of Light. Without talking about it, and perhaps without being noticed, they are important to every spiritual community.

The first thing that I heard from these Friends is that it takes a really long time to grow up. We have this idea that you become an adult in your 20s. You go out in the world, make some decisions, and make your own way. Do you remember the story about the young man who thought that his parents were so dumb? He left the farm and went into the city to make his own way, and he had a hard time doing it. He came home a year later and he was shocked to find out how smart his parents had become.

Friends told me that if you were lucky, and did your homework, you would be awake in your 60s; if you worked really hard, maybe in your late 50s. But if you are really going be awake, if you are going to live in the Spirit, you have to wait until later, because it takes a long time. It takes a long time to get a broader view, to get more discernment. It takes a long time to get out of your own way.

One lovely Quaker woman told me about being able to flip perspective within your mind. If you had a strong feeling about something, maybe about a group of people or a situation, could you have the flexibility to think about the people on the other side of the line, or the other end of the equation, and seek to understand them, to have mercy and compassion for the way they understand the circumstance? Learning to do this in a regular way took a long time.

I was also given the idea that you could grow past that ongoing question of "why me?" If you stick around long enough and surrender to the Light, apparently the answer to that question becomes: "Why not you? You were standing here like everyone else. It's your turn." What a lovely simplicity!

Friends also told me that they had come to a lovely place of being "tired of righteousness." I'm speaking of the righteousness of the loud, passionate thumping of the chest, which is full of ego and has very little mercy and compassion. They told me that this came largely through the luxury of time. When we are young - working jobs, taking care of children, and tearing around the world doing things - there really isn't very much time, there isn't time to wonder.

Other Friends said that it's lovely being the patient observer: sitting back rather than doing, getting the overview, watching, maybe doing a few small important things behind the scenes, becoming very important glue in ways that people generally didn't notice.

Most of the Friends I spoke with expressed no fear of dying. Two of them said directly, "Oh, there's lots worse things than dying." I remember a lovely old Quaker lady in my meeting in Putney, Vermont, who was approaching an "old" age. I asked, "Alice, do you want to live to be a hundred?" She said, "I just want to stick around as long as it's fun." In helping hundreds of people who were dying in the AIDS epidemic, I found that to be the most perfect criterion in the world - just stick around while it's still fun.

Friends also expressed to me how their concepts of God changed over time. As their spiritual life deepened, they found that there was almost no human-made presentation or representation that fit their understanding of God. One woman said to me, "Now that I have time, I have done a lot of reading, mostly spiritual books. I've been reading about other religions. I find that I have a bigger idea and fewer words as to what God is. And if I told the other people in this retirement home what I was thinking, they would run away screaming. It's just gotten looser and more wild and has less and less to do with words."

When my grandmother was a little girl in Italy, she confessed to a priest that she had considered calling her mother a bad name when she was angry one day. The penance the priest gave her was to drag her tongue along the floor from one end of the church to the other. This was when she began to understand organized religion. Her ideas of God became much clearer and independent of the church.

Another big topic was humility. It seems, if you stick around long enough, you get to think about your place on the landscape and other people's places on the landscape. Many Friends said that one of the markers for the deepening of their spiritual life was that they had less judgment of other people, less judgment of themselves, and more mercy. They also had a better capacity to set aside those parts that did not honor their best, to rearrange themselves for different groups so they could fit the place they were needed. They became more aware of the quality of surrender - not giving up - but finding a flow, finding a Divine tide and surrendering to it.

They also talked about the idea of being more comfortable with oneself as a fool. Maybe we don't intend to be a fool, but certainly we have all have lots of personal examples to work with.

For myself, in preparing to speak to you today, I thought of all the foolish things that I have done as clear and concrete examples. I ran out of paper on the third day.

One of the things these old Friends talked about was humility and how much we don't know; realizing that what we don't know is much larger than what we do know. When we are pushing, when we are insisting, it might be a good idea to keep in mind all that we don't know, which remains fairly large no matter what our age.

They especially mentioned that the deeper their spiritual life became and the longer they were here, the less specific their prayers became. One might ask for certain outcomes in one's 20s and by one's 50s one feels a sense, a tone, a reverence that surrounds the matter, a very different form of prayer.

As people grew in their reverence, and in their familiarity with the Light, prayer became less and less specific. Rather than showing up with a demands list, as they grew in the Spirit, they came to feel a tone of reverence, a tone of the Divine, and to sit next to it and let it envelop them, and not be stuck in the idea of getting across a list of needs and wants.

They also described a very strong and clear effort to try to balance the understanding of personal competence with humility. We want to own what it is that we are good at, and at the same time keep track of those things we don't know well, and keep both of these in mind as we go along.

They expressed the idea of coming to Meeting for Worship with no expectations, surrendering to the Light, not trying to get something particular done, no pushing, not coming with a full agenda, not making demands.

Another strong idea is what I call "Light time". There is a rhythm and a pattern to life, movement and flow, which we can rarely see or understand from the perspective of our own egos. There is a synchronicity of events unfolding, and it takes quiet observation to see where you fit into this plan. There is Divine intention. If you make your spiritual life deeper - your capacity to notice the timing of the Divine, to listen more deeply – this perception will grow. Our capacity to trust how things are unfolding and how it is we should be involved in that flow – these also become larger. We notice when way opens and when way closes. This is very often a nonverbal sense. It takes a fair amount of stillness and a fair amount of quiet, and again, that luxury of time for wonder, for noticing, for being close, for feeling how something is changing, maybe within us and maybe around us.

One of the ways this sense grows is that we notice what has happened in the recent past. What have the patterns been? What has changed that we notice when we look back in retrospect, retrospect being a very important part of the study? What has already taken place that informs us about the next part of the pattern?

Something else that Friends are very clear about is that insight feels good. It feels good to wonder and to come to a greater understanding of yourself or a greater understanding of the Divine. It feels good to see how we are all aspects of the Divine, how we are the breath and the fingers of the Divine, and how easy it is to lose track of that insight.

One Friend was very clear that it is very important to work with self-confidence rather than self-esteem. Her sense was that with self-esteem we are much too dependent on compliments, perhaps making us vulnerable to betrayal. But with self-confidence we have a clear idea of what we are capable of doing with our work. This is an understanding that comes from insight, wonder, and experience, over time.

Spiritual experience was a very large topic in our discussions. Friends felt very clear that exposure to events that draw us deep into the Spirit, opportunities to hear vocal ministry, presence at a gathered meeting, were priceless for deepening the spiritual life. To experience - especially among Friends and our tendency toward the mystic, to feel how finite our minds are and to feel how infinite the Spirit is. Words are insufficient for what we see, know, and come to understand as normal and regular. This learning needs to be experiential; it's not what we think. One Friend said, "Isn't it just impossible to explain to someone what a gathered meeting is, what a covered meeting is? There just are no words for that."

There was also comfort in ambiguity. We understand the Divine in many ways, some of which are not even compatible with one another. It might be that the ways Light is presented to us in our early life make less sense as we become adults and other ideas come later in life. Some of these are contradictory, and there might be some things that we believe and feel, but we aren't actually going to know until we get back home to headquarters.

To be comfortable with ambiguity is to be comfortable with the idea that there are concepts and ways of feeling and thinking that there is no language for, and that there may not be a way to decide what the nature of God is. To be patient with that ambiguity is all part of mature seeking and the simplicity of knowing that there is much that cannot be known for sure.

One Friend said to me that he spent most of his time outdoors because that's where he found Meeting for Worship to be most powerful. His understanding was that the highest place a person can get to spiritually was to be in awe of creation. There is a very tidy design to the universe, and if we are in awe of the creation, it brings joy to our bodies and our minds, and we have a sense of well-being. We participate within that creation in a way that is gentle and constructive.

Friends also talked about childhood visions and visitations as adults. Having visions, having a visit from the Spirit world, tends to be a private thing people don't talk about very much. People often don't understand its meaning or become conscious of it until later on. That's very common. One woman told me that when she was in her 50s, she was taking a yoga class at an ashram. She was chanting in Hindi and she had a very clear visitation from Jesus. While she was chanting, she asked Jesus, "Do you mind if I am stepping out of Christianity to do this?" and Jesus replied, "No, I couldn't care less. I'm just glad you show up."

Another Friend told me about a time when she had eye surgery, back when eye surgery was done in very crude ways, and she had to lie in bed without moving her eyes for weeks. One night, Jesus came to her very clearly and spoke three messages to her: "Love ye one another. My grace is sufficient unto thee. Bear ye one another's burdens." She suddenly understood that no matter what happened to her, she now had this action plan that she could live into for the rest of her life. She didn't have to worry about what the outcome would be. She was filled with Light. She is one of those very special power generators. When you sit down next to her, you just feel better because she has no doubt about the nature of God. She has no doubt about her connection. It's an ongoing thing that she feels continuously.

Friends spent a long time talking about the practice of spiritual life. Mostly they said you have to show up and let it work on you over a long time. It accumulates in you gradually, over time, and it accumulates in the body. This is one of the things that I particularly like about Quakerism; it is a somatic religion. It is a religion that we experience through our bodies. We feel our bodies change as we center down into worship. There is a change in our breathing, there's a change in our posture, there's a change in the amount of tension we have and are holding in our bodies.

One Friend said that she was very grateful that she had found Quakers. She now had a context for seeking in one specific way rather than to keep seeking for ways to seek. It meant that she could put time in one groove, make a home, and polish that stone to make it shiny. It's very different from going from one thing to another.

Another Friend said that spiritual life has to be habitual. We have to make it a habit of mind to be in contact with the Divine, to have mercy on ourselves and other people, to respond compassionately. There has to be a decision somewhere along the way that we are making this choice, and we are going to make it a regular practice.

Then there clearly was the idea of fidelity, which means showing up on a regular basis. Don't just say you're going to do your spiritual life, show up and do it. Get down into the quiet. Find the prayer that brings you deep, and get there regularly. This is a regular practice before big work with ourselves or someone else. Find what's best for us and engage in a regular way.

Some folks mentioned having a Spiritual Friend, someone they talk to and make conscious their experience. Other folks talked about the importance of community, especially for grief and for celebration.

It's also important to have a role model, guide, or mentor, someone who can help us see that there is greater depth to the experience than we currently see, someone who welcomes our seeking, and has the deep calm and the hospitality for our seeking.

Another topic came up that was a surprise to me. Friends talked about betrayal as an event, a situation that could help deepen our spiritual lives; something extremely painful, where trust is broken, when there has been a trespass or abandonment, when something is so painful that part of us dies. If we can still speak our truth, if we can maintain our integrity, betrayal will teach us that Light is the main reality. Examined troubles teach and failures teach. After trouble, we learn more deeply.

One Friend said to me - only one - "I have no experience of betrayal."

After trouble, after grief, and after convalescence - sometimes illness feels like a betrayal of the body - it might be that we have less fearlessness. Maybe we use that peaceful time to rest and to wonder. Convalescence might also be preparation for moving on to a next plateau. There was some laughter around the idea that we never seem to welcome trouble, but we do learn what its uses are.

~ ~ ~ ~

In my work, healing from trauma is sacred learning. Can we gather up all of our calm, and all of our compassion, and sit down next to the monster without trying to kill it, without being afraid? Can we share a nice cup a tea with the monster and understand what it means?

Now, there are some obstacles to growing in the Light and becoming an old Quaker smoothie who schleps the Light. One of the problems is that our culture is very busy and very noisy. It is violent, materialistic, and dishonest. You really can't go too far in American popular culture without running into some of that. There is a very large cultural push for us to be the same, for us to be similar to each other in profound ways. We watch for those obstacles and see how to sidestep them. Early Friends talked of being *in* the world but not *of* the world. Do we have ways in which we separate ourselves from the culture?

This brings us to a topic that Friends are especially good at: eccentricity. After this study, my experience is that old Quaker smoothies who schlep the Light are a very peculiar bunch of folks. This is not unusual among Friends, as you know. It turns out that this eccentricity, this quality of being different from the usual or the expected, is absolutely vital. Sometimes in our spiritual life we have a tendency to keep it private, maybe because we think it's going to be embarrassing. As a result there is a great deal of spiritual experience that remains unheard.

I suggest that we consider enjoying our eccentricity, enjoying our difference, becoming more of who we are. Don't bother to put our Light under the bushel. Enjoy and grow those qualities in ourselves.

I want to repeat that these qualities may not be something we should all strive for, hoping that we all become these old Quaker power generators, that we all become Quakers who schlep the Light. This is a rare condition. But watch for it and become aware of it, because it's very important to our spiritual life.

In this time, when there is such war mongering, and so much suffering, and such waste of resources, it is absolutely vital that we find and hold on to our roots, and stay close to the Light.

As for myself, I hope that I live and study long enough to become an old Quaker smoothie who schleps the Light; I would love that. But as I look at how many mistakes I make each day, and as I remember my dear friend who is 90, say "It takes a really long time to grow up," I am relieved that I have a long time to study and that nothing is going to happen quickly.

Old Quaker Ladies

June 2007

Bill Kreidler, in his 1989 keynote to Friends for Lesbian and Gay Concerns, used the image of an "old Quaker lady" to denote a life lived so much by doing good works that its connection to spiritual experience becomes common and ongoing.

I have some ideas about old Quaker ladies. I know this won't be easy. Some men will cry foul and say I'm romanticizing women and leaving men out. Let me say simply, that after 25 years of trauma work, touching bodies in hospitals, prisons, church basements, and torture survivor treatment centers, it is abundantly clear to me that testosterone is a chemical that says DO while estrogen is a chemical that says BE. Any transsexual can explain this if need be. All spiritual life begins with being. It's not men's fault they are doing it in reverse order and it takes some time to catch up. Nor, goodness knows, does this mean that anyone gets a free pass without tons of homework.

Spiritual experience, like all intimacies, is cumulative. It shows up, every day in whatever context you choose to frame it. It brings the elements of time, practice, discipline, and effort that together create a tone, a glow. It moves and has power, inwardly and outwardly. To be old has value in spiritual life if one has shown up and practiced over a long time.

Another element is surrender, handing over control to something larger than yourself. It is setting the self aside enough to avoid hearing yourself more loudly than the sounds of the universe. It is yearning to see, and understand, and be in awe of creation. Being in awe is the highest spiritual posture.

Being is engaged before Doing. In the long-term work of spiritual intimacy, I would like to suggest that old Quaker ladies - assuming their disciplined seeking over time - have a place in the Religious Society of Friends' spiritual movement that is little recognized and should be more utilized. In short, they are spiritual power generators. They are beings one can count on to lay the spiritual grounding in the times and places where there is deep seeking and there is need of reverence and the absence of the logical mind with all its silly obstructions.

I recall at Friends General Conference Gathering in the late 1980s, I set

up grieving circles for a few years as so many Friends with AIDS were dying. It was a terrible time. We had few viable medicines, the onslaught of diseases was not understood, and gay men in the US were dying by the thousands. I was able to lead these grieving circles, but I needed spiritual backup. Who would have the spiritual muscle to hear with me these untold stories of overwhelming grief and help guide the process in reverence? I invited Muriel Bishop, who had recently begun her prison work. Prison chaplaincy had given her a depth of strength and trust in the Spirit. She was in her 60s, which was very useful as I was only in my early 30s. While this was exhausting for both of us, she swam in the deep waters gracefully.

Later on, I was in Toronto at the home of Nancy Pocock. Refugees were told she was the person who would help them find asylum. Nancy's house was overflowing every weekday morning and afternoon with people from Central America, the Middle East, and Africa, each with a horrible story of what they had survived. She was in her 70s and 80s during the years we worked together. I asked how was it she was not overwhelmed by all that was asked of her. She answered in her usual slow way that sometimes left an impatient person tapping their foot. She thought she knew the limits of what might be possible and she only did what she could, which turned out to more than she first thought possible, and much more than others would dare. She understood that she was not awash with urgency but rather in a slow dance with the universe; she assumed no grand notions of herself, cheerful to have a calling of some passion, and moving at the pace and style she needed. She would have been happy to continue as a jeweler, but this was more exciting. When the time came that her heart was deciding to finally quit, she lay on a gurney in the emergency room calmly writing a letter on a clipboard to help one more refugee.

Elizabeth Watson, in describing her writing process, told me there was a necessary amount of stillness and wonder to engage without specifically seeking any one idea. Then, suddenly, she had to write. In writing her book, *Wisdom's Daughters - Stories of the Women Around Jesus*, she learned that she had to clear an uncluttered space in her mind, apart from her knowledge of theology and ancient Greek, and ask that the stories be revealed to her. She used a similar discipline when she gave piano recitals of in Bach. Elizabeth wrote and taught into her 90s.

The elders for the Quaker Initiative to End Torture, QUIT!, were carefully chosen. These five old Quaker ladies, mostly lesbian, had been around the block and knew the difference between a form for reverence and reverence itself, and between good work and discussions of good work. They knew that holding the spiritual ground while hearing horrifying stories was a natural match for their age and experience, a perfect fit for what needed doing.

Quaker men, of course, are not immune to the accumulation of Light, given decades of spiritual practice. David McAllester went to the Navajo nation decades ago as a young anthropologist seeking to record traditional daily life, especially music. After a time, he became so desirous of the essence of their gentleness – in such stark contrast to American culture - he sought to enter their society as much as possible, rather than simply observe and record. Into his 90s, David helped Friends understand reverence with his being and his elfin smile. Even his walk radiated the power of gentleness.

These stories are about the essence of being, the stillness in which one listens for the Light. Knowing that the clearness for and holding of the connection between the person and the Light is primary work. It is perhaps the most important part, whether or not something more follows.

I often suggest to young Friends to choose an old Quaker lady to sit next to in meeting for worship and see if they can feel her sinking into prayer. When you choose well and have enough of your own stillness to sense another's spiritual disposition, the experience is unmistakable. We have old Quaker ladies and gentlemen for just this purpose - to feel what accumulation of spiritual seeking is like, to feel what decades of regular practice amounts to, and to have a better sense of where we sit on a landscape that has many elements.

Doing may be the most obvious. But being, and particularly surrendering, is the larger, less obvious underpinning of the entire Quaker experience.

I once proposed an Old Quaker Lady Contest at Pendle Hill to set right the vibrations of a new building. No one took me seriously. The fact is the vibes were set right by an old Buddhist lady and her class sitting in long, deep, meditative reverence for days.

Simple Complexities

August 2009

It happened again recently, and, while it is not frequent, it is not unusual. I'm at a yearly meeting and a woman comes up to me. She says that in the past few days she has realized that whenever she is standing near me that her neuropathy stops hurting. She laughs and says that since she can't take me home, I will just have to give her extra to last as long as possible. We both laugh, and I give her a long hug while humming a deep bass line, perhaps like a very old refrigerator, or maybe a dump truck, pretending that I was delivering the extra requested. We laugh again. She says thank you and I say it's my pleasure or it's my honor.

In this simple exchange, a few givens are acknowledged. She feels less pain when near me, and we both know this is neither talent nor technique but a spiritual gift that comes through me. I have some responsibility, but ultimately I'm a mere tube for some Light to come through. I have the task of being a good tube. This includes acknowledging that this gift is not from me. It is not mine but rather a blessing with origins beyond me. Like much of spiritual life, it is beyond words of simple description. It is my lot in life to learn and use and be faithful to this gift.

Some people will hear just that much and conclude I have relentless ego or I think I'm divine. Others will say it's illusion, imagination, or simply bizarre, meaning it's beyond their own spiritual experience. Part of what will be missed with such dismissals is that I understand the hard work involved in the discipline of such a gift. I am not important in the transaction, by which I mean the great thing here is the Light itself, of which we are all aspects. I am as separate from that Light as anyone, even as I work to learn more about it.

Some disciplines required by the work are not understood. The first is solitude. The intimacy and intensity of having another's pain pass through you is not common. It's beyond empathy. I need solitude to recover and refresh from the work. It means I need to rest, away from others, even during a conference. This can appear to some like a prima donna taking herself too seriously, but without an office or office hours how else does one stop work? Once I am in whatever village I am working in, I'm on. I don't stay in the village and say no to opportunities to work.

Saying no is work too. Rather, I live and rest at the edge of the village and come into the center when it's time to work. This life at the edge and the need for solitude is even less understood than is the gift itself. I am still learning, after all this time, the disciplines of opening, closing, washing, and resting. Once grace withdraws, then I am alone, trying to do my best as just any other person, and as lost and found as any.

Early Morning Light

February 2009

I haven't put this story to paper before. I understand it differently now, maybe in ways I couldn't have decades ago. It was early morning when the phone rang. A woman I'd taught with in prisons was calling. She'd just come back from the hospital with a young friend who had been raped earlier that morning. Could I come do healing work at the survivor's house now?

I shower, dress, and leave, in a haste of bodily motion, but in my mind I am quiet and prayerful. "Be thou with me as I do this work. May I be a vessel of Light." It is a long drive, giving me time to go over what I've heard, and then set the details aside to reach my deepest calm and feel the heat grow in my hands. I tell myself, "No worries. No fear. Don't interrupt the given flow of Light with mere human obstructions. Ride the high tide to deliver the best."

She had been out late at a party. Walking back to her car in a dangerous part of town, this small young woman was literally picked up and carried into an abandoned building by a much larger man. She struggled and was beaten. When he was done, he walked off, leaving her in the dark and cold. From the police station, she called her friend. They met at the hospital and now they both were at the survivor's home.

I come in slowly and quietly. I need to see and feel her response to this assault before I begin any work. Is she so tired and weary that she is calm, or is she fretful? Is she still or pacing? Are words still too much to process, or can simple, slow conversation happen without too much pressure?

She is in pajamas in the living room. Showered and exhausted, she's been given a sedative but hasn't really slept. We don't discuss particulars. She feels best close to her friend and not talking very much. She lies on the carpet and we begin. I keep my hands soft and my touch firm. I touch only her head and limbs and do not approach the areas of trespass. I've done this work more times than I can count. Sexually abused women make up the largest group on the planet. But before this time, my work always came years after the assault, not fresh like this.

There are no words to describe how it feels to open yourself to feel another's pain come into your body. There can be no flinching or wincing or partial acceptance. It is beyond story, or listening to wailing, or witnessing desperation. It is beyond empathy. It is a wave of knives forcing their way through, and any resistance catches like fishhooks. The task is to come in calm and strong, stand and face the wave, feel all of its meaning and dimension. Then, let it go through - the bull under the red cape, the car sliding sideways on ice, the grief of trespass, brutality, and disrespect, all without filter.

I touch her head and shoulders. I hold her feet. I hold her hands and draw down her arms. Each of these touches is a "Hello" and "can we connect essential energies?" Mostly it feels like an empty garage, only a shell. But by and by comes that energetic response in her of, "Yes, I am here," and soon a flood of her essence pushes to the surface. I draw this out, as one would unfold a large tablecloth underwater to find the stains that need soap and scrubbing. More and more comes to the surface. "Show me all there is."

She is still lying quietly with little expression, no sound. I am working up a sweat doing simple touches, all the heavy lifting is felt and not seen until - towards the end of the work - I am sweeping my hands over her as though I am gathering up all the Light around her body. I am scooping up her most immediate and intense self to raise it upward, heavenward, for cleaning. This is when tons of grief lifts from her body, passes through mine, and is released. My face crumples with terrifying sadness as my arms stay aloft. Her rage and deep sadness wash through me and are gone in moments. The friend sees this and identifies it accurately later. The survivor goes off to bed to sleep peacefully.

I have a long drive home in which to be in awe of these moments, the work of being faithful, and doing more somewhere soon. I'll see her for the first time a decade later. She will thank me again and I become teary to hear her gratitude and remember that early morning Light.

It's now more than 20 years later as I write this. Looking back, I can see this miracle, not of my making, is what I had wanted for the first battered woman I knew, my mother. Living with unrelenting violence and no one to provide protection created a longing in me. How this longing became connected to warm hands that lift wounds out of the body is beyond my understanding. It's a terrible gift, terrible and beautiful. Terrible, because there are no gloves, save focusing on the Light. It cannot be done except in the war zone of that person's trespass. It's beautiful, because relief is witnessed over and over in the most splendid geometry of balance and rightness. The process and understanding has changed for me over the years, but the basics remain the same. Gathering enough reverence beforehand is crucial. Rest and quiet afterwards are important, too. I've made a small, good life that allows me to dip into the gruesome. The older I get, the more beauty I need to balance it.

Light Carried and Shared

Pendle Hill Lecture Series May 2013

I've been teaching at Pendle Hill since 1990 and it's always one of my favorite stops when I'm traveling.

Tonight I want to share a few stories with you and do some readings from my first book. I want to talk about following a leading and listening for your call. Probably one of the most important things to keep in mind is that no ministry is born whole. Things start out small, and in bits, and so they might be missed.

There was a young lawyer who wanted to fight injustice; he went to law school and was at the top of his class. He found a very obvious case of discrimination and went into his first trial. The case was very clear, and he should have won it, but he lost. He lost because he was too shy to speak in the courtroom. That was Mohandas K. Gandhi. Isn't it wonderful that he didn't stop there, that he kept going?

There was a wonderful person in New York City. She was a homeless girl - all kind of ragamuffin - and she wanted some money for new clothes. She heard there was going to be a talent show and thought she'd go and dance. When she got to the theater she found out there were so many dancers signed up that she probably couldn't win. So she thought she would sing instead. She came out on stage dressed in rags and people laughed at her. When she began to sing, they say it got so quiet that you could hear a rat pee in cotton. That was Ella Fitzgerald. It's a wonderful thing that she kept going.

There's a story of a young writer at the MacDowell Colony. She had just started a book and was very discouraged. She was talking with a friend and said, "I don't know where it's going. It may just be empty. It starts out with a letter." That was Alice Walker talking about *The Color Purple.*

It might be, as we are listening for our calling and listening for a leading, it might be so small, and so subtle, that we miss its small beginning. We should watch for it closely, and tenderly, and with a gentle focus.

When I began, my work sort of snuck up on me. In thinking about the beginnings of my work, I remember little spots along the way that were hints for me.

I think there were many small beginnings, signs along the way. Helping my cousins soothe the pain of nettles at age five, being a young person that adults confided in, being able, early in my life, to feel in others a larger sense of their emotional life than they might be conscious of - I now see these as pointing to a possible future in healing work.

But there was a particular time I think of as the point when my healing work really began. I'd had some tutoring in massage and was soon to enter massage school, but hadn't had formal training as yet. I was thirty, and a good friend complained of a nervous stomach. She wasn't sleeping at night, was often nauseated, and couldn't keep food down. Doctors found no physical cause for these symptoms. I offered massage.

As she lay on the massage table, I slowly worked over her muscles. She was a strong, athletic, young woman. When I came to her belly, I felt a rush of emotion move through me. My hands became very warm, and she began to shake a bit and later to weep. Soon she told me she had suddenly regained a memory of abduction and torture as a young teenager. There were burn scars on her body revealing old abuse. She began to feel better soon afterward, but then, of course, had to work with this new knowledge.

This kind of experience began happening to me, but I didn't know what it was. I didn't understand it right away. It actually had to happen several times over the next few years before I got a clue. Sometimes I got the feeling that my angels are sitting up there on a cloud around a card table saying, "When is this numbnuts going to start paying attention? We send him all kinds of clues. Could he please look up?"

~ ~ ~ ~

Let me talk a little bit about choosing work. Probably the most common question I receive is, "How do I find my work?" Friends are very conscientious about attending to what work they should be doing in the world. This is one of the things I love about Friends. There is an expectation that everyone should be on some sort of spiritual adventure and it should involve engaging the world in some way to help lessen the pain and confusion in the world. I love that about Friends.

Here are a few thoughts about considering ministry and work and leadings. Lots of folks think they should be drawn to the biggest crisis or the most urgency. I think those should be considered, but more important is what brings you the most Light, what work would be the best teacher to open you into your best self.

There's a tendency for people to want to rush in to save the world, and I suggest that the work we are doing is not actually saving the world, which to the best of my knowledge is really a very long vigil. We do compassionate work, peace and justice work, work of healing and helping, to come closer to the Divine, to help reform our own interiors, to know the Light up close.

Some folks try to do the absolute most they can, and stretch themselves to their limits. This is one of the reasons that my anti-burnout workshops all across the country are very popular among Friends. We know that piece very well. I suggest that what we really need is to be doing our best, not our most. Our best is wonderful. What does your best look like? How does your best need to be supported? That's what we need to be doing.

I also suggest that we attend to our own healing first, to awareness of need for our own healing. Making our lives clear is our first work and gives us lots of information to use in our work in the world.

Likewise, the work we do in the world gives us wisdom useful for our own healing. These two points of healing inform one another all the time. The work we do out in the world is something we use for our own interior healing, and the work that we do on the inside informs our work out in the world.

~ ~ ~ ~

Here is an idea that is easily misunderstood and often gets me in trouble. God is not some guy.

Often, when we're in trouble, we start praying to Big Daddy God to take care of everything. We claim that we are helpless, and we know nothing, and since "You are in charge of everything and You are the landlord who owns everything, (who really is a very big grouch and who you should not anger because he will fry your butt,) will you please help me?"

We forget that we are aspects of the Divine, that we are the fingers and the breath of the Divine and the Divine is not some guy. But rather it is an ocean of Light that we can step into with our awareness at any time, and every time we remember. We are part of the ocean of Light. This is very easy to forget as soon as the troubles begin.

It is important to remember that everyone has pain and no one is superior. There are mindfulness and faithfulness or there is forgetting. We are all of us doing our best. (Uh oh, this is my best? Oh, are we in trouble. Yes, right now this is my best.) Can I be merciful with myself? The more mercy we have for ourselves, the more mercy we can have for someone else.

There is no honor in joining someone else's suffering. The honor is in carrying the Light. The Light is strong, but as carriers of the Light, we are fragile, and we must be very careful as we make promises, as we engage, and involve ourselves. Let's choose work that stretches us, but does not overwhelm us.

Let us do work that is hard and also fun. I think of fun as part of the grounding mechanism. We have to be able to find some humor, especially in the mistakes we make, especially in the things we are not very good at, and then attend to them very carefully and see if we can get better at them.

This is a letter that I wrote some time ago to the *Brattleboro Reformer*, our local newspaper, when I was having some fun:

"Another lovely August 26th. We are enjoying our sixth wedding anniversary with memories of that special day. Almost two hundred people gathered to hear our vows. 'In the presence of God and these our friends, I take thee to be my husband, promising, with Divine assistance, to be unto thee loving, faithful, and a delight as long as we both shall live.' Quaker elders from across North America joined us, their faces beaming at this traditional wedding. Students and their parents from schools where we worked were there, too.

"But our reverie was interrupted by a letter in the *Brattleboro Reformer* from someone claiming to be a Christian minister and pretending to inform readers about gay people. Imagine, a fundamentalist preacher writing about gay people as though he knew something of his topic. We suppose there are Wall Street bankers who have gardens, but we wouldn't ask one how to run the farm, for mercy sake!

"In the spirit of one misinformed turn deserving another, allow us to tell you about fundamentalist ministers. Historically, this is a group that began when the Coney Island shows ran into hard times. There were a number of midway barkers, those men who shouted outrageous claims about what's in the tent. Their job was to draw a crowd by telling half-truths and bold lies. They sold tickets by getting people excited or scared. At the turn of the century, there were terrible layoffs of carnival barkers. These barkers were a skilled but lost tribe. There were only so many jobs in newspapers and insurance. So, what could they do?

Religion was their best bet. After all, their voices could reach the back row of any tent. Plus, fire and brimstone were not so different from tales of bearded ladies with tattoos and sword-swallowing midgets who ate glass. Some vocabulary changes were called for, but the tone was similar.

The trickiest part of this new vocation was that there was no one for the crowd to stare at and evoke chills. This called for more theater than before. So, instead, they explained who was a threat and why. Since people are always looking for a good scare, this worked like a charm. The easiest part was that it could be more fake than any beard. The list of who it was okay to hate began to grow like Pinocchio's nose. The barker/ministers meant no harm; it was just a job. Now, decades later, like many movements, they have forgotten their roots. They take themselves and their stories seriously.

This has never been much of a problem in Vermont before. Historically, we know the difference between a ghost story and a town meeting. We don't confuse compost with harvest, nor rumors with knowing. But lately there is this terrible noise claiming to be knowledge. Vermonters don't like badmouthing people. It's not Christian. It's not a good way to live. Life is too short. Summer goes by too fast and neighbors need neighbors.

Beware of preachers who insist on telling you what is true and who the bad guys are. Our anniversary is a true story."

~ ~ ~ ~

When I was settling into my work back in the early eighties I realized how difficult it was going to be. I was doing lots of work in the rape crisis and began doing lots of work in the AIDS epidemic. I remember sitting in prayer and saying, "This is going to be really hard. Is this really what You want? You want me to do this? It's going to break my heart over and over. How can I do this and keep going?" The message came back clear as a bell "Your main job is to stay tender."

So, how do we stay tender? We must make beautiful lives for ourselves, ones that we want to live. If we can do that, it helps us remember how beautiful and good life is, so we can then go and do the hard work. Tenderness is something that we often reach by remembering how important it is to lay down the weapons around our hearts, to lay down the weapons of the ways that we think about other people or other circumstances. How is it we can be tender with ourselves and then also with other people?

One of the things I learned about staying tender is that there are a lot of necessary and fierce disciplines. You know that in order to relax a muscle, you have to exercise that muscle. You have to wash and feed it and take good care of it so that later on you can lie still and relax and be whole. I have arranged and organized my life around being faithful to my gift. It happened slowly, over time, but the more I surrender to it, the smoother it becomes and the better I am used.

There is the problem of ego. There is the problem of thinking you are important. There is the problem of feeling powerful. And there is the problem of other people putting you on a pedestal, other people thinking that you are powerful.

Questions and Answers

Q - I was wondering if, in your ministry, you found it at all difficult in your relationship and how you deal with that?

A - Well, my husband, Marshall Brewer, is very well connected to Quakers even though he was raised Methodist. He has blood relationships to Susan B. Anthony and a half dozen other famous female Quakers in his genealogy and he knew a great deal about Friends when we met. He is involved internationally doing compassionate work.

Very soon after we met, he experienced what my healing work was like. Very early in the marriage he said, "I commit to you that I will take work that will help you to do your work wherever it is you need to go." So, there is that understanding and recognition, and he has been there to help me through every piece of work, not only traveling and teaching around the country for the last 30 years, but also to begin The Quaker Initiative to End Torture - QUIT! Then he was there to help me finish writing the first book, which for me, as a dyslexic and learning disabled person, was very hard work. He is an excellent editor and has pretty much read everything I've ever written. It's not only true love that I celebrate every day, but also the loyalty and dedication that I hold for his work, too. He has two masters degrees and I propped him up at the computer through both of them. There are times when he reminds me that I need more rest than I'm aware of. When I work too much he reminds me. Sometimes I have the choice to stop and sometimes I don't, and the same is true for his work. There's a lot of dedication there.

Q - Can you tell us a little more about what is helpful to people in great pain?

A - For all of us doing compassionate work, the first thing to keep in mind is that pain has function, and the function of pain is learning. When we take the trouble that we see and study it, observe it, and watch the parts, we can actually learn how it is constructed. If we remember that all trouble, conflict, and pain, is for learning, then we can find a way to approach it. When we intend to help someone who is in a great deal of trouble and pain, it sometimes is pain that we are not familiar with. It might be a kind of trouble we haven't experienced. In that case, we might be working more theoretically, but the mindset is the same.

I bring my care and strength and calm into your circumstance, and I am a witness to your experience, and I will be with you. First of all, I do this so that you are not feeling alone and, secondly, so that you can share your deepest truths, and, to the best of my ability, I will not be frightened. I will not become as frightened as you are when I listen to your story. This is a very beautiful gift.

From there, we begin to piece together what's needed, what's the next step, what can be offered, what isn't known that can be found out, what support and help can be brought in. Remembering that pain is for learning is the first part.

It is important to be fluent in our own pain. If we know the pain of our own lives well, understand it, and have worked with it, then we have a lot of gifts to bring to someone else. I came into a lot of pain very early, so my education was quite complete - really by age seven - so I was getting ready to go to work very soon.

Q - Can you talk about forming the Quaker Initiative to End Torture and how this fits with the other facets of your work?

A - Did you know that for eight years I was a Montessori teacher with young children? I thought I would do that forever. I loved it. The kids were great. I liked them better than adults, and they liked me better than adults, and we just had a great time. I'm still in touch with some of those kids. Some of them are now doctors and lawyers and judges. God help me, I'm ancient. I thought I would do that work forever, and I didn't realize that it was preparation. When I began working with rape survivors, I thought I'd be doing that forever, and then the AIDS epidemic came along, and then I did some work in prisons, and then some with tortured refugees. Each piece has been preparation for the next.

When pictures of Abu Ghraib came out, I called all the major Quaker organizations and said, "We need to have a conference on torture. This is work Friends need to take on the way we took on slavery and women's suffrage. This is very important." All the organizations said, "You are absolutely right, but we do not have the time or the money or the people. If you start something we will help you." So I called five friends, sort of the way one calls five kids in the neighborhood to say, "Let's build a tree house!" They said, "Yes, we will work with you to do this." Within a year we had a listserv, we had publications, we had our first conference. We've had four conferences now, three in the United States and one in Canada. We have videos posted on YouTube that can be reached from the QUIT website.

One of the important things about the United States of America is that its promise has always been very great. People want to love their country. People want to love their country like the great mother and have those promises fulfilled. We've had a sickness, a duality. Torture has always been against the law and we have always used it. Despite the public pronouncements, American torture continues today. It has not ended. It has not stopped. It's important for Friends to know the stories of American torture, both the history and the current circumstance, so that we can share those stories.

There will come a time when there will be movement in government, for investigation and story telling and prosecution. If you think of all of the wars that the United States of America has sponsored around the world - the American war in Vietnam, the American war in Nicaragua, the American war in El Salvador - all these were fraught with American torture. No one above the rank of lieutenant has even been charged, much less tried for these crimes. It would provide a great healing for the United States of America if the leaders who made the decisions to use torture and who continue to use torture were brought to accountability. It would be a great healing for our country.

The United States of America is at once a great sanctuary for millions of people and we are also the McDonald's of torture. We studied torture, experimented with it, and perfected it. In the last twenty years, torture around the world is no longer done in traditionally ethnic or regional ways. It is done the American way. We have taught the world how to do torture. This is a great work for Friends to take on. It's a nearly impossible work, which we're very good at. It is long-term work; it will take at least two generations of Quakers to accomplish it. That's also something that we've very good at. It is also good work to take on because it is abhorrent, and it is obvious.

Q - Isn't basic training in our military where training for torture begins?

A - Both of my brothers were in the American war in Vietnam. There's this great dichotomy in the military tradition. Many, young people go into the military and stay for their career because they believe in honor. They believe in fighting for justice and fighting honorably; that one follows the rules of war, and fights honorably and fairly. This was one of the reasons that American torture was outed. Honorable military people were disgusted by the use of torture. This is one American atrocity that is ongoing.

The other reality is that when you train someone to fight in a war zone, you train them to respond without thinking. This is absolutely necessary. This is not a matter of respecting someone and negotiating; it is a matter of fighting to the death.

These two things have lived side-by-side forever and both of them are true. There's that lovely old saying that you cannot prepare for war and peace at the same time. How do we train someone to fight efficiently in a war zone, and then not have them take that mindset out into the world?

This is a mystery that has never been solved. We are stuck with it now. We are stuck with thousands of veterans coming home from two wars. In the last four years the rates of suicide among soldiers and veterans have grown to be greater than losses from combat. Those who are not killing themselves might be killing their spouses, or killing their children, or beating their families. Essentially, the problem is that war is unhealthy. It's a lousy system, a lousy choice, and it makes everyone sick who is involved with it. We don't have a healthy way to run a war and we're not going to.

Q - How are you able to practice humility in such a public life?

A - One of the difficulties is that those working for healing and peace and justice rarely admit how difficult the work is. We rarely acknowledge how difficult it is - to work in prisons, to work with the military, to work in war zones or former war zones. We rarely are honest about how much it hurts to do the work. The conundrum is that we need a lot of support; we need a lot of help. The people around us are saying, "I thought you said the work wasn't that hard." There is a lot of Light and it does support, but then one must lie down and I haven't been able to get to my bed for the last three days because of the reports I've had to do. We need to acknowledge more that the work is really hard.

We also need to learn more about the body and how to use the body, because Quakerism is essentially a somatic religion. Messages come through the body, and we vibrate within our bodies, and use the Light and use our bodies in the work. We need more body awareness - this is my bias as a massage therapist. How can people quickly rest and relax? Do you know how to do that? It can be done, and you better learn it because you've only got five minutes.

We need more space for grief. We need space for people to be weary and to grieve the losses they have witnessed. Quakerism is a British form, and that stiff upper lip to stay calm and carry on - well; we're pretty good at that. As an Italian Quaker, I've been holding up my end of the screaming. It is painful to live in the United States, with all of our electronic media feeding us all of this information of disasters all around the world, corporate dominance, genocide, unsafe drinking water, thousands of babies dying each day. It is hard to absorb all of this and not have time to grieve that humanity has not gotten any better. Is there anything new in corporate domination since the Dutch East India Company? Only that it's gotten worse. Have the wars changed? No. War is a dumb idea that someone comes up with, and it usually has to do with someone's money. If we're going to be aware and awake, we must see that the losses we experience are gigantic. We need to have more space for grief, and for rest, and for restoration, so that we can then do the work.

Q - What do you think of the political system?

A - In 2005 I began a regular practice of reading newspapers. At about nine o'clock, I tuck Marshall into bed. I read him the restaurant review from *The New Yorker* and he goes to sleep in about three minutes, so I can use the same review all week. Then I go to the computer and spend the next two or three hours looking at 10 or 20 news sites. I have 30 bookmarked on my computer. I look for stories about torture. My view of the American political system, after reading the international press, is the following - you will not see anyone in leadership in the United States of America interrupting corporate dominance. Anyone who wants to interrupt corporate dominance is not allowed into the final races. I wish I could say it was different, but if you look at what is being said, and what is being done, the differences are especially startling.

Recently we noted the twentieth anniversary of the release of the "*Pentagon Papers*". Keep in mind that everything that Nixon was to be impeached for is now legal. President Bush, President Clinton, and President Obama have all been part of dismantling civil liberties. They do this while they claim to do differently. I wish I had something better to report. I wish there were a reality that could challenge that in a way that I understood. But I don't see anyone getting in the way of what corporations need.

Q - Is there a way to respond to the pervasive abuse in our culture?

A - Whenever we go to war, there is more rape, domestic violence, and violence in general in our country. We have been at war longer than ever before, and in more than one place. The incidence of rape always increases in wartime. The culture of brutality, and meanness, and stupidity, and that the tough guy should win, dominates. We can't run a culture that way and hope to have it be a good and beautiful and long-lasting society.

One way to respond is to begin with yourself and to be clear about the pain and burdens in your own life. Become aware of the pathologies around you that affect the people you know and love and are engaged with. Try to understand how that works. Are you engaged in naming that, in not contributing to that? Are you trying to understand it, and help others understand it, and so take energy away from it?

Then you might want to take a look at a larger picture. But not a picture that is too large because it will exhaust you. Too much information is available to us. I could read reports every day about children dying because there is not enough clean water in the world, but if I did that every day, I wouldn't have the time, or the energy, or the heart, to do my work.

The challenge in our media age is to distinguish between how much information helps us understand and move, and how much discourages us. There's a lot of work put into keeping people frightened and discouraged, so choose our sources of information carefully, and choose the amount you take in carefully. Let's think of the long-term; we can choose a piece to work on now, and save other parts for later. The part that we choose should bring us a great deal of Light, should help us keep our strength.

Can't See the Path

October 2013

Advice given to a young friend with a calling to healing work, but worried that he can't see the way forward.

Dear Friend,

Good question, two part answer.

Knowing one has a calling is a special condition. It's fine to feel passion, excitement, and even a bit stoned in the experience of the work. But ultimately, confirmation of the calling comes from one's community, those being served and those who witness you, perhaps elders. Watch to see who you are talking about this with, who understands the feelings and the skills. Do you understand it in a spiritual frame? Do you have a sense that a gift comes through you? Do you sense that you are special in a way others are not, and that this can be a danger?

In its beginning, healing work can feel like one has fallen in love. It's very heady and delicious. This is true in part because the work itself is done mainly beyond thought and without linear thinking, though hopefully with a full sense of anatomy, physiology, and pathology as much as we can know. The primary guidance is not from knowing, but from sensing - from receiving messages that build our awareness. As we surrender to that listening, we are in awe of what is. Now, that's a neighborhood anyone would want to be in lots of the time. But our disciplines must be to go there for seeking, sometimes in service to others and sometimes for our own learning. It's never stealing a smoke behind the barn, but rather, always a holy place that one enters with reverence, never casually, but over the years more and more smoothly.

As for seeing the path - wanting to know how the story is going to go – that is very Disney, very American. But we are not supposed to know where it goes, how we'll be used, what learning will take us where. It's the adventure of a lifetime, a whole lifetime. Everything that has happened so far is part of the ride. And we must keep track of where the ride has taken us so far, and what we've learned, and what we wonder if it's still true. Then, we keep track of our heart's desire - where we think we'd like it to go - while realizing, even though we do make some choices, we are not steering. Every group of tutor angels, or ancestors, or animal totems, or however you think the cosmos is organized, are placing things in our way for us to choose or not, to obstruct or proceed, and all of it is for learning.

Sometimes I thought I'd work on a cruise ship. Sometimes I thought I'd run my own school to teach people how not to die. This was clearly my bias at the beginning of the AIDS wars and wanting so many friends to live and my being afraid of death. Sometimes I think that after 31 years my story is mainly over, nothing new to witness. And then BOOM! New stuff comes and new learning comes and all I know is I am used again but in new and different ways.

So, no, you are not supposed to know what's next, at least not very far off next. It is only in the rearview mirror that we see how it is all connected and made sense. Of course, we worry about it, and we think there should be a plan and we should be the ones choosing the plan. To some extent we do, it's not all a roll of the dice. By and by, we begin to choose out of our knowing and not out of our wanting.

We are not supposed to choose the hardest work, but rather the work that will polish our Light best. We are not here to do our most, but rather our best. These often look very different.

OK, enough lecturing. That's what you get for asking such a good question. I trust you know most of what I mean and the rest will come.

Section 3

Goodness

About Your Goodness

I want to think about goodness in three ways: as an original constitutional part of each person from their beginning, as something we learn in the experience of living and making choices, and as a developmental aspect of being human that is life-long and reveals more as we age.

From their beginning we see goodness in children as a natural response to others. As a Montessori teacher with young children, I saw goodness as the most common element in all children. For eight years I saw the many ways goodness is expressed in 24 children, three to six years old, at eight o'clock in the morning, - even when snow suits and boots were the largest part of the curriculum. They might forget what's right or wrong briefly, but they always remembered when action was halted and they had a moment to ponder.

It's quite rare for people to have neutral feelings about their own lives. From each event in our lives we draw some meaning as to the nature of the world, of others, and of ourselves. We can think of goodness as a deeply held understanding created by how it feels to be in the world, the messages life gives us, and, most importantly, how we respond to those messages. Our response to life may either bring clarity or add to the pain and confusion of life. It is a developing perception and an ongoing process. There is an element of time and moving through one's life. There are major influences of nurture and cruelty, loneliness and belonging, and shame and delight in life.

Time, experience, and the meaning we derive from it all is that which brings knots, contentment, brokenness, and exhilaration each day, every moment through decades.

And whatever might I mean by goodness? I mean knowing in your heart that you are essentially good, that your faults and mistakes are not the sum of you or even a fair representation, but rather that life itself is beautiful, though difficult, and you are part of that beauty and the wonder of all creation. I mean that goodness is a generosity of spirit within people that is seen in response to themselves and others, when they can clearly see the defenses caused by fear of scarcity.

Maybe time brings us various periods in our lives that teach us different

things. When our life changes, does our response to it and our understanding of it also change? Will late adolescence teach us the same lessons as childhood? Will old age contain the same messages and experiences as middle age? Do we recognize consistent themes? Do we sometimes understand something new from an old story later on?

There is commonality to many of our experiences. We learn the culture of family and extended family, school, work, independence and dependence, freedom and it's absence. Most of us experience these. At the same time, very important experiences can vary and our responses to them can be equally different. The child experiencing violence or love may or may not derive the same meaning from it as the late adolescent does from similar experiences. The fabric of one's life is a fabric akin to others, but it always is individual, separate, and different in its parts.

I think our experience of our own goodness comes from working to bring balance to our understanding of, and responses to, our various experiences. The materials we have to work with are a large library of experiences and a broad view of possible responses, along with the honesty of our gut feelings. Hopefully, over time, we learn to balance our various responses to better fit the situations we find ourselves in. The first flat tire or the first falling in love perhaps elicit very different responses than the next time or the fifth time it happens to us.

The power of important life experiences can build up a particular perception over time. Doesn't disappointment in love or success with money gather a meaning all it's own in our lives? Don't we come to think of ourselves in a particular category of life as either being gifted, deprived, useless, ignorant, blessed, or mysteriously missing something in some way or other?

I think that, over time, our positive experiences give us an identity that we hold with some awareness. On the other hand, our negative experiences are held lower down in our awareness and gather hurt around them and so, perhaps, there is a reluctance to view them honestly and openly.

This might lessen our knowledge of our disappointment and the area of life in which it takes place. Could disappointment turn into shame, perhaps blaming oneself? Could the lack of understanding of the moving pieces of a situation bring us to hold that lack of knowledge in a way that maintains our ignorance?

Moving into the realms of our disappointment and misunderstanding, trying to find and experience a positive outcome, can shift our knowledge and change our understanding of ourselves and also of the experiences.

Does the car wreck and injury to the body mean pain, trouble, disability, and overwhelming costs in all ways, or might it also mean an opportunity to respond with strength, perseverance, receiving help, and being grateful to be alive?

Does heartbreak mean another spiral of loss, depression, and grief without understanding, or might it also mean one is in a state of learning, preparing for the relationship that works well and is actually loving?

Here's what I want to suggest – we come to know a sense of our goodness by learning to consciously control our energies and deliberately bring balance and flexibility to our thoughts and emotions, and then bringing all this learning into the choices we make in the world.

When we learn to balance our strength and power with compassion and mercy - with our selves and others - we open the door to knowing our goodness.

When we balance our fear and anger with knowledge and self-discipline, we relieve the patterns of blame and useless explosions, providing room for peacemaking.

When we balance our grief and shame with the knowledge of the beauty of life in ourselves and others, and are in awe of all creation, we give balance to our place in a vast landscape and remove the focus that powers guilt, replacing it with hope.

When we balance our isolation with the experience of good village life where each has a chance to become their best self, we set the stage for giving and receiving in the flow of life.

How, then, do we accomplish all this in a single lifetime? Good question. I am writing about numerous moving pieces, some of which seem perpetually out of reach, and others that can seem like complete strangers. What can I possibly be thinking? We are not all sitting on a hillside watching the clouds make pretty shadows on green fields. I know. Neither am I.

Here's the simplest way I can express it. Our sense of our own goodness comes from essentially five experiences and these experiences can be chosen, invented, created, and lived, as ways to make new patterns and bring new experiences to life.

These five experiences are sources of knowing our goodness:

- A regular pattern of giving and receiving of love

- Use of our personal power for the common good

- Taking stands of conscience

- Keeping the rules that we make for ourselves

- Awareness of the Divine/creation/nature

Giving and receiving love

The experience of giving and receiving love in an ongoing relationship is our first food. This sets in motion our sense of goodness, knowing the beauty of connections with the world and our part in it. Over time, we come to know the moving parts, the problems and obstacles, the delights and highs, and the patterns of success and failure in loving. But our strongest personal connection to goodness comes from the love we trust and the love we delight in giving in our personal life and in the world at large.

Personal power for common good

Using our personal power for the common good is a step into good village life where we experience goodness as compassionate response beyond our immediate needs. It extends us out into the world, even if only a little bit. When we contribute to the common good, we begin to take our place in the moving mandala of life, choosing to be of help, experiencing some personal power, gratitude, delight in the dance of give and take.

A stand of conscience

Taking a stand of conscience is a more extreme form of using our personal power for the common good. It's more extreme because it is accepting personal responsibility and stating that some correction is needed and we are choosing to be part of the steering, not merely an observer. When we say, "NO! This cannot be allowed to continue," or, "YES! We want this to stand as is," as a response to injustice, that's when we decide from our sense of right and wrong the direction we know to be correct, as much as that can be known at one time. Experience teaches us that such declarations can be corrupted and mask illusions, such as using biblical passages to justify slavery. But on the whole, beyond personal, selfish choice, a stand of conscience teaches us where integrity lies, the nature of the culture we live in, and what society does with dissent in any form. This is true in families as well as nations. It is a large education that puts us in contact with peers and companions necessary to continue, as well as opposition that will surprise and inform us beyond our seeking.

The rules we keep

There are rules we try to adhere to that also shape our lives. Some of the rules have been laid upon us and others we have made for ourselves. We consciously and deliberately find our goodness in the rules we choose to live by. There are rules that sneak into our being that offer little and are great burdens. These do not feed our experience of goodness and might be dropped. Let us consider the rules we live by and think about how these can be points of reference that relieve us from repeating regrettable mistakes. It's a relief to look back and know that the mess we once made in our lives was a part of pattern we stepped out of and haven't returned to. These rules provide a comfort and a structure that we rely on as a good part of our reality, a part we maintain for good reason.

Being in awe

Each of us has experiences that put us in awe of creation, of the beauty of the universe or of the Divine, depending on how we understand and define these larger realities. That moment of witnessing a birth, the love that saves our lives, the stunning beauty of nature or great art, the moment of contact with other worlds - all these humble us and connect us to something greater than ourselves.

They help us gather a sense of goodness in ourselves. They suggest that we are part of this grand parade and are a witness to its being. We can make good use of this experience of being humbled. It saves us from thinking too much, and especially of thinking too much of ourselves. To see a forest fire or surrender to a Beethoven symphony is to know just how small our personal selves are in the presence of these great forces. These reset our perceptions in a way similar to having a good night's sleep or rebooting a computer. They give a bit more balance to how we think. We feel a part of these things that are grand; this helps us to know our own goodness in ways that the more humdrum day might not.

Spiritual experiences vary in depth, intensity, and definition. Moments of grace, where fear and want fall away, are not only impressive but also addictive. That moment of seeing some part of creation that puts us in awe can be too rare; it feels so good, we want more.

All of these experiences - of love, helping the common good, acts of conscience, rules we make and keep, and experiences of awe and the Divine form a network that lifts us up toward a better self over time.

Obstacles

There are obstacles to our finding a sense of goodness within ourselves. These tend to be common and may be sneaky in day-to-day life. But we can watch for them and see the patterns of interruption they bring.

Pain –

Perhaps the most common obstacle to a sense of goodness is pain, particularly ongoing, long-term pain. This might be physical pain such as joint or nerve pain from a chronic condition, or it might be emotional pain from long ago events that have never been resolved. Pain is exhausting. Long-term pain wears down our energies. By and by, we often assume some guilt or fault for the pain we carry. These conclusions might not be conscious but often lurk in the background, blocking experience of our goodness. Pain can be an obstacle to hope, trust, and creativity. We may no longer be able to imagine any way that things can get better.

Vanity –

When we have more concern for how things look than for how they feel, we may block honesty, truth, and our capacity to be clear. Shielding ourselves from what is real takes energy away from honesty; it takes what might be a sense of goodness and makes it artifice.

False Humility –

When we are thanked for good work and respond with, “Oh, it was nothing,” but on the inside we are thinking, “That was a hell of a lot of work and you have no idea how much I sacrificed,” then we are putting up a false front. Some may see this as polite, but it disallows the ownership of our achievement and accomplishment. When we do not own our power and do not celebrate and delight in good work well done, we sacrifice the experience of the natural flow of good hard work, well done, being seen and recognized, by ourselves and others. Wouldn't it be better, instead of saying, "It was nothing," to say, "You're welcome!" with heartfelt delight?

Shame –

Shame is the first, natural response when we do the wrong thing. We are naturally ashamed of hurting innocent people, stealing, lying. Unfortunately, it is also the pivotal point where one can experience the most manipulation from another, and is a familial and societal tool taught and used, to the great waste of human potential. In so many situations, shame is laid upon people to gain and keep control over them. It can be the veneer of interpersonal or institutional communications.

Shame also arises when we are overpowered, when we cannot protect ourselves from assault, insult, others forcing our bodies or lives to be used in a bad way. This is the humiliation that comes from bullying.

When we carry shame, whether laid upon us or from our past actions, we doubt our sense of goodness. When we cannot admit our wrongs, we interrupt our sense of goodness.

Perfection is not required to feel our goodness. Shame sometimes feels like an interruption of our integrity. Often such feelings are carried in secret, making it all the more difficult to bring it in to the Light. Waiting for perfection is a long wait. Those things for which we have actual, credible shame need to be brought into the Light to be observed, washed, and surrounded by mercy for all affected. In this way, shame can be healed.

Antidotes

There are antidotes for these obstructions and they are reverence, honesty, and clarity in one's sense of self.

Reverence –

Reverence is knowing that something is very important and must be treated quite carefully. There are some things we recognize as being very special and needing to be held and cared for very carefully. We know that something is fragile or powerful and deserves to be handled with extreme care, such as an infant or trust. Having reverence for our own lives keeps us from making casual choices that obstruct our sense of goodness. Choosing carefully enables us to keep things in good order in the paths we choose. Reverence reminds us what we know is important.

Honesty –

To be able to say clearly, "This is how I feel," or, "This is what I see," or, "This choice will lead to X," is important for living well and fully. The lack of honesty corrupts our connections to our sense of goodness and cast doubts into already complex situations.

A Clear Sense of Self –

We probably already have a pretty clear idea of who we are and who we are not. But do we allow ourselves a broad enough scope so that we can bring in new and growing aspects of self, thus allowing us to become our best? When our worst is shown to us, can we do more than recoil in horror? Can we know that whatever may be true at the moment, that it is not a complete picture, not the end, of a work in progress? Can we become accepting and comfortable with what we have done wrong and what we have done right without the drama of excess guilt or excess kudos for our actions? To see all of ourselves, the parts and pieces of the whole, and know that life is still becoming, and that we can do good, is the clarity that washes away the obstacles to a sense of goodness.

Life Map –

My Life So Far

For this exercise you will need:

a large piece of paper - even better would be a blank, opened, manila file folder

a colored pen/marker/pencil; or a set of different colors, one for each of the five parts

The Horseshoe Chart

Position the paper vertically. On the paper draw something similar to a horseshoe with the open part down.

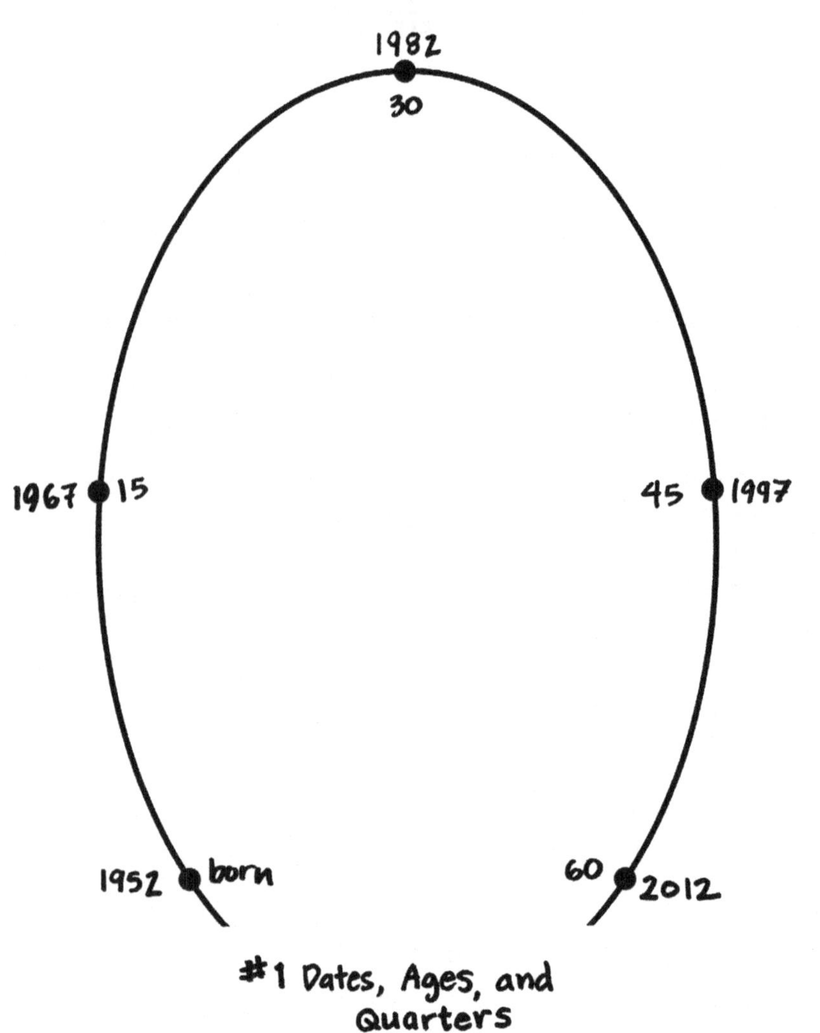

#1 Dates, Ages, and Quarters

Dates, Ages, and Quarters

Look at the diagram above. You can see that at the left bottom of the horseshoe, I put the year I was born: 1952. Put the year you were born in that position on your chart.

At the right bottom of the horseshoe, put the current year and your age. I am 60 years old. The year is 2012.

At the top of the horseshoe put your half-life and age. If your half-life is not an even number, put either year that represents half of your life. I was 30 in 1992.

Half way up the left side, put the year and age that represents the first quarter of your life so far. I was 15 in 1967.

Opposite that, on the right side, put the year and age that represents the third quarter of your life. I was 45 in 1997.

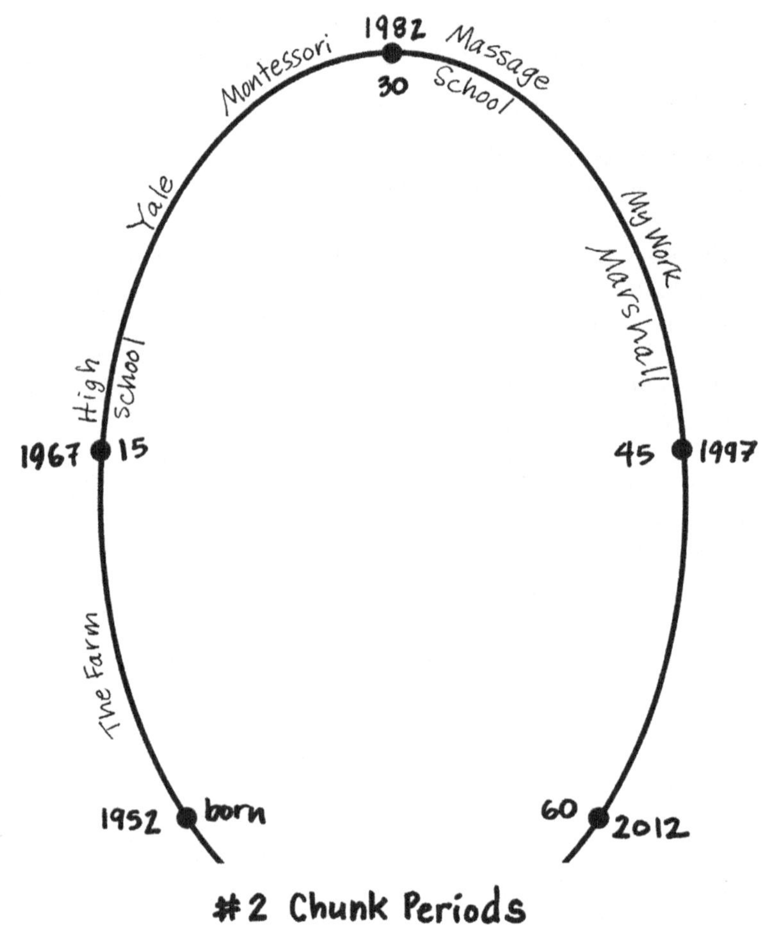

#2 Chunk Periods

Chunk Periods

Now for each quarter period of your life, think of your life in chunks, periods of your life defined by where you were and what you were doing or maybe those you were with. Make it very simple and start with the most inclusive characteristics of that quarter of your life; the first large impressions you have when you think about that time of your life. If you have more than one chunk for the quarter, put them in chronological order moving around the horseshoe. You may want to lay the words along side the line rather than sticking out.

The first quarter of my life I have named "The Farm." My mother's parents, both born in Italy, bought a farm in a little New England town in 1925. My mother, the oldest daughter, grew up there and she was given a parcel at the north end of the farm where pigs had been raised in former years. This made the gardens around our house very fertile indeed. In my early years there were three households on the farm and the rest of the family didn't stray far. I grew up in a beautiful New England country landscape with dozens of cousins. I learned to milk the cows when I was seven. I started learning to drive the truck when I was ten. I carried firewood for my grandmother every winter day in the last years of grade school.

Move on to the next period and define the chunk or chunks for that period, just a few words.

The next really different and distinct part of my life was high school, from 1966 to 1970. For a shy, scrawny, gay, dyslexic teenager, there are few things worse than high school in a little Yankee town where the 60's revolutions hadn't shown up until about 1970. My friends Mel Ash, Martha Fell, and I were the Moratorium Committee, protesting the American war in Vietnam. Two other friends and I began the Folk Music Club where we played guitars and sang folk songs. I taught swimming at a 4-H camp each summer. Learning disabilities were just being invented, so I missed the boat that might have explained high intelligence and low grades.

The next part of my life, 1970 to 1974, I was at Yale University in New Haven CT. But I've said I had low high school grades; how can this be? Well, I worked on the loading dock and was not a student. I had a Conscientious Objector status from my draft board, a CO, and this job would be my alternative service if I got a low draft number. This was at the height of the war when my two older brothers had already served. I was there four years, even though I got a high draft number. These were my college age years and there was a lot of unfolding and becoming while living with groups of friends away from the farm.

Then came my time of being a Montessori teacher 1974 – 1982. I trained at the Whitby School in Greenwich, CT, and worked with young children, 3 to 6 years old. I had wonderful and generous mentor teachers along the way. I loved it. I thought I would do this forever; maybe even start my own school. I also taught guitar, banjo, and dulcimer at Killooleet summer camp in Hancock VT. This work began to slowly transform me into a disciplined professional, and a critical thinker. When my time teaching young children was over, I felt that most of my brain had been located and had begun to function well.

In 1982 I left teaching and went to massage school in Boulder, CO. I graduated in the spring of 1984 as a Certified Massage Therapist specializing in trauma. This was my grand awakening. In the process of learning massage, I released a great deal of early childhood violence and trauma, and therein found the true nature of my life's work. I worked with my first trauma client in 1982 and discovered my gifts in compassionate work as a healer. In 1984, I began to live mainly on gifts, and work by invitation, and that has continued to this day.

I met Marshall in Vermont on the last warm day of summer in 1986. We moved to Los Angeles for his work that winter, and to Washington, DC, the following winter, and then back to Vermont in 1990. It is his love and good care that has anchored me in ways that allow me to do my best work in the world and find sanctuary at home.

Complete naming the periods of your life in each quarter to date. What you have at this point are the periods of your life laid out in order around the line.

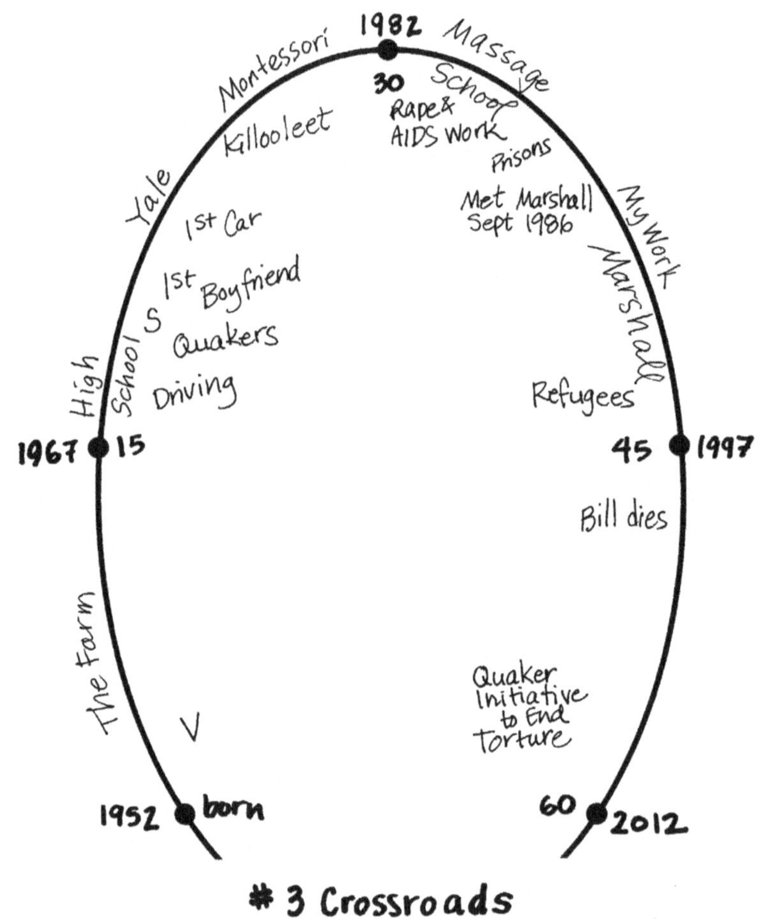

3 Crossroads

Crossroads – important events

Next, I make note of important, life-changing events in my life. Maybe it is something wonderful, like first love or getting a first car. Maybe it is something terrible, such as violence or a loved one's death. I wander through my memory of each quarter, looking for those important times when something happened, and for good or bad things were suddenly different, life had changed.

First Quarter

In the very early part of my life there was a great deal of violence, so I mark it with a V. At 14 I write 'music' because I began to play the guitar, and compose, and I would perform as soon as possible, probably too soon for some listeners. Music became a large part of my life, my identity, and my work.

Second Quarter

I got my driving license at 16 and discovered two things - I love to drive, and there was a Quaker meeting in the next town. These are two things that have been delights in my life every day since. So, at 16 I note Quakers and driving. Then, I put a big S because I attempted suicide at 17 and never told anyone until years later. I had my first boyfriend at 18 and realized what all the love songs were about. But my second boyfriend was a better kisser and the importance of this became very clear. (Here I note Al and Richard.) I got my first car when I was 20, and a new Martin guitar when I was 25 – this, more or less, was all I ever wanted at the time. I began teaching as a camp counselor at Killooleet summer camp when I was 23. This was a great place for a young adult to grow up and learn education from the inside out, along with being the best place any kid could spend a summer in the Vermont mountains.

Third Quarter

One of my songs was performed and recorded at Carnegie Hall. I was 30 when I began massage school, a decision that changed everything in my life. I began doing working with rape survivors and in the AIDS wars. I discovered my life's work, and met my true love, my husband. That would be enough right there. But it went on. I began teaching in prisons and working with tortured refugees. I moved from Colorado to Vermont to California to Washington DC and back to Vermont. I began living in a little house in the Vermont woods surrounded by forests and farms.

Fourth Quarter

I helped my best friend to die; he had AIDS. We bought our house. I experienced a period of healing deep, old anger, during which friends were lost. We celebrated 25 years of marriage. I became the founding convener of The Quaker Initiative to End Torture - QUIT! in 2005 and thus began years of learning and teaching about American torture so that Quakers might join all efforts to end this policy and practice.

Add the details of important life changes to each quarter.

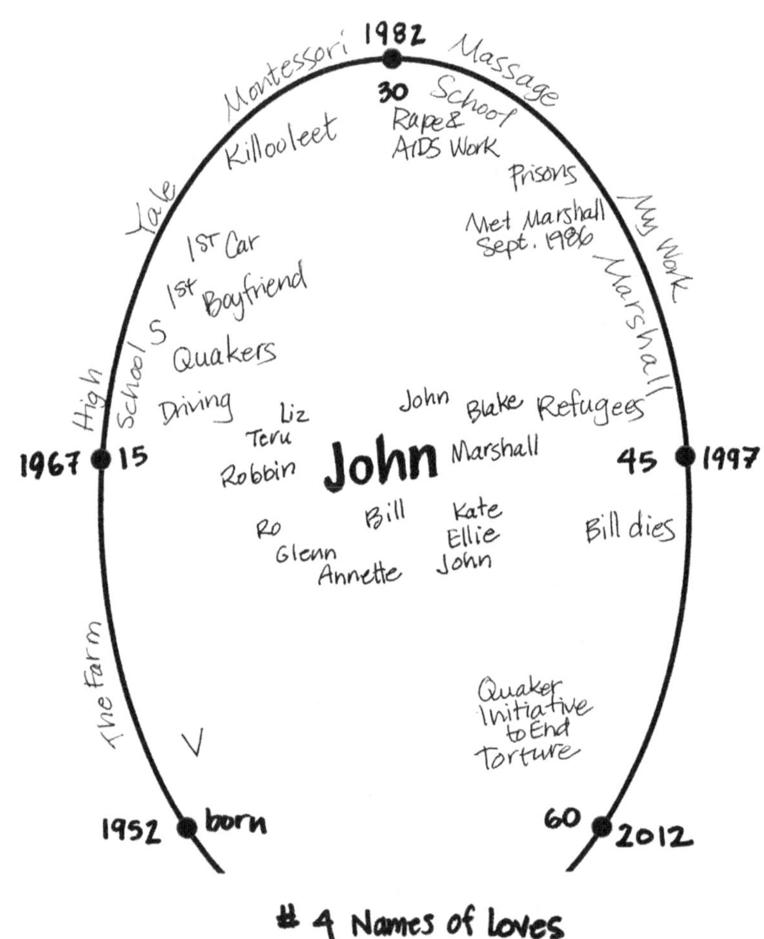

4 Names of loves

The Names of Love

In the center of the chart I write my name. Then I think of the people I feel closest to, the people whose love I trust and find credible. I write their names near mine, and the closer I feel to them, the closer I put their name to mine. If I don't feel very close to them, I put their names a little further from mine. Often, I only have about eight or ten names. I am surprised to see how much change there is over time. The circles we move in - co-workers, family, co-conspirators, romances - are often in motion.

Doing this part of the chart at the beginning of each new year often reveals subtle changes.

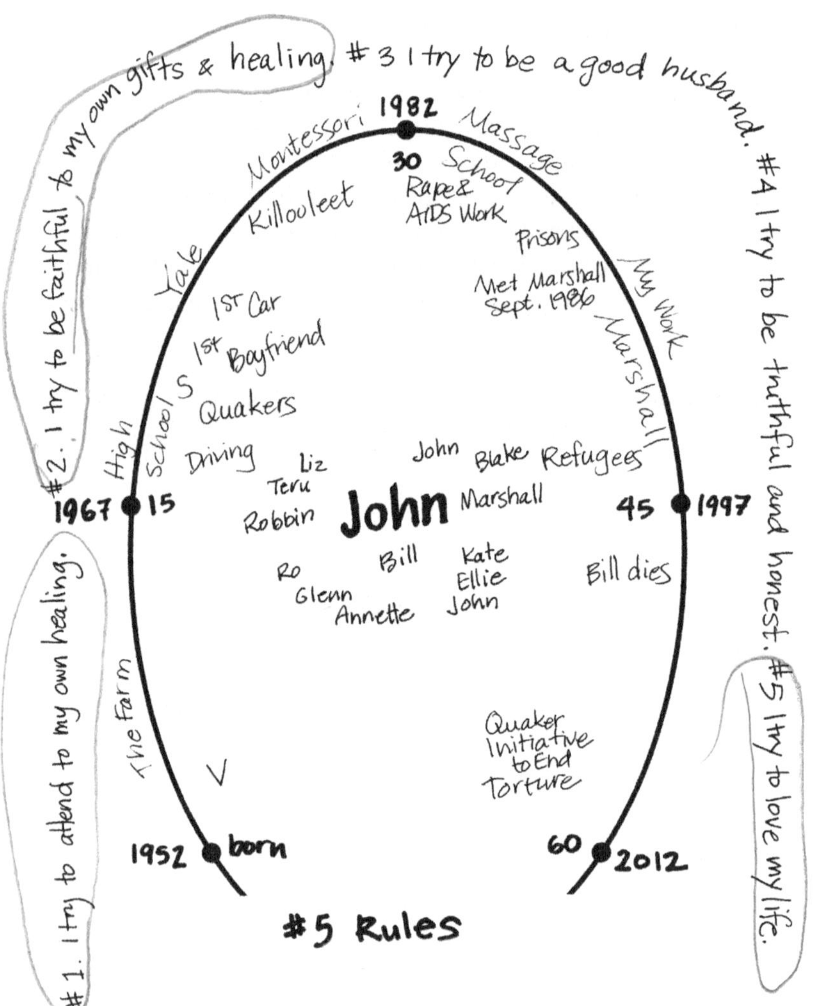
#1. I try to attend to my own healing.
#2. I try to be faithful to my own gifts & healing.
#3 I try to be a good husband.
#4 I try to be truthful and honest.
#5 I try to love my life.
1982
30
Montessori
Massage
School
Killooleet
Rape & AIDS Work
Prisons
Yale
My Work
Met Marshall Sept. 1986
1st Car
1st Boyfriend
Marshall
High School S
Quakers
Driving
Liz
John
Blake
Refugees
Teru
1967
15
John
Marshall
45
1997
Robbin
Ro
Bill
Kate
Ellie
John
Bill dies
Glenn
Annette
The Farm
Quaker Initiative to End Torture
V
1952
born
60
2012
#5 Rules

The Rules that I keep-

Now, along the outside edge of the chart I write down five rules that I've made for myself that I try to keep. These are the ways I try to live, remembering what is important, and keeping in mind what comes first when I make important choices and organize each day and year. The tone in which these rules are made - You Must! or You Should! or I try - says a lot about the tone you use with yourself and how much structure and mercy you allow yourself. This, in turn, reveals the mercy you have for others. A complicated history of screwing up and making bad choices may call for more structure than others. Does the structure hold tones of guilt and shame, resulting in rules wounding you with each application? Are there rules we use, rules laid upon us by others, which we have not consciously chosen? Do these serve us well? Do you hear someone else's voice doing the insisting - and it's actually a voice you don't like? All this can take some pondering, and changes can always be made. Write down the rules you use to keep your life on the path you want to live.

Here are the rules I choose and work with after all these years:

- I try to attend to my own healing.

- I try to be faithful to my gifts of healing.

- I try to be a good husband.

- I try to be truthful and honest.

- I try to love my life.

Want! makes us aware
of how I critically need God!

How I need to reach in
deep inside
I need this place of deep reaching & hunger for God.
In the midnite
I am so lost from this
& I realize it... then I reach!

What a lovely experience – If I am not afraid
to face & feel it. The tenderness of
this need – this reaching
down into darkness
for God.

Finding the Five Sources

Now comes the hard part. Often, we think our lives are ordinary, nothing special as compared to other lives, we think our lives include some good, some bad, some struggle, and some gifts. But if we think of each day in our lives as a series of amazing triumphs for the young person we were, and brave endurance in the life we live now, then maybe we can see that no life is ordinary. Our life becomes a unique accomplishment, an achievement that only we could have done. Our obstacles, our gifts, our strength, our failures are like no one else's. Each and every day of our lives are known completely only by us, and no one else.

For this exercise we need our best introspection. We gaze into our own life to remember details of feeling and experience. We seek out those times when we had the chance to feel our goodness, as seen in our actions. Pondering the whole chart, let's look for evidence of each of these five experiences.

A Regular Pattern of Giving and Receiving Love

When in our lives have we had love that flowed, was easy going, was love that we came to count on? Maybe it was long lasting, maybe it was short term, but it was enough to let us see and feel what might be possible. Mark the chart, or write a journal entry, or tell someone of the times when we have experienced a love that taught us what love is. Looking back, what were we being taught about love and what expectations of love or of ourselves were created at that time?

Using Personal Power for the Common Good

When did we do something that helped others and the only payback was knowing that we did the right thing? When did we help another with something that was important to their life? Are we more given to small daily help or to larger, long term help? Have we done something grand or dangerous? Are we known as someone who helps? Mark on the chart, or write a journal entry, or tell someone, of the times in your life when you have used your personal power for the common good. How was your life shaped and how did you feel about yourself after these experiences?

Taking a Stand of Conscience

There are times when something is going wrong, some decision, or tradition, or law, is causing injustice. This might be within the family, or at school, or in a public arena, such as the justice system. Have there been occasions when we spoke up about unfairness as a matter of conscience? Was there an event where we worked to create change or opposed a decision because it was wrong? What were the forces opposing us? Who was helped by our taking this stand? Mark on the chart, or write a journal entry, or tell someone, of the times in your life when you took a stand of conscience. Did all hell break loose? What else happened?

Rules We Make and Keep for Ourselves

Do the rules you've made for yourself increase your trust? You may ask, "My trust in what?" Good question. Rules that honor your best intentions, limit your weaknesses, and offer broad possibilities for your achievements increase your trust in yourself, your judgment, your ability to make good decisions, and enable you to face the challenges you encounter in the world. Rules that nag, insult, or remind you of failure do not honor your best self nor help you trust your perceptions of self or your sense of the world. Those rules cause a loss even before the first steps are taken. Mark on the chart, or write a journal entry, or tell someone, of the times in your life when you have made rules for your self or changed the rules, or why you have chosen the rules you have.

Divine/Creation/Nature

I remember seeing the Grand Canyon for the first time. There are no words, of course, for seeing a landscape beyond imagination and beyond what one's own mind can fathom. It is beyond what can be understood simply by looking. One gazes at it, overwhelmed and stunned by its existence. I was humbled and in awe of its immensity. My eyes had to range, and travel, and return left, and right, and down, and up, trying to see all that was in front of me.

Being in awe, truly stunned by beauty, by rightness, or by raw power, is a very particular place to reach in human experience. Whether we are in awe of great art, or a frightening storm, or phenomena understood to be spiritual - it's good for us to be stripped of the limits of our hum-drum existence and have our senses wowed by the great unusual that cannot be easily seen, or understood, or replicated.

Mark on the chart, or write a journal entry, or tell someone, of the times in your life when you were in awe of something much greater than yourself. Did the birth of a child increase your reverence for life? Did the view from the mountaintop help you to know how ordinary valley life can be? Is it possible for you to seek those moments of awe as a way to keep a perspective on a life that refreshes?

Summary

Goodness can be a part of our awareness, part of our experience. We can seek it more completely and we can employ it therapeutically. Pondering our lives, where we've been, what we've seen, as a way to keep contact with our experiences and have all of the knowledge available may remind us of our competence and how much we know/have achieved.

The life map you create in this chapter can be referred to over time and added to. The more we remember, the more memories come. The more individual parts become clear, the more connections between them appear. Then we begin to see a whole. Our wholeness and how it came to be is a grand door to healing. This is something I hope for all of us.

Flagstaff deep need in 2007

Huntsville 2012 - Love & Mercy for own experience

self-acceptance love of individuation of students

← Kayenta 2008

Section 4

From *Friends Journal*

Six Healing Sayings

May 1988

I had begun to wonder whether what I was doing was at all useful. We had been working for more than an hour.

The stillness in the massage room had become thick. The soft-music tape had run out and the candle had burned low.

She lay on her side. I placed one hand over her heart and the other at her mid-back. "Take a breath," I said, quietly. Soon all we had worked for was achieved.

Her chest and belly heaved twice. Her face tightened and the sound of old pain broke the air. She wept with her whole body, soaking the sheets and exhausting herself. She purged an old hurt, which could not become history until it had been released.

The quiet following the storm was both clean and full, not unlike a meeting for worship at its best. She accepted a glass of cold water and a box of tissues. Gazing out the window at the Vermont greenery, she asked, "What do I have to learn to stay this clear?"

A good question. Laying down the weapons around the heart is one thing. Getting them to stay down is another piece of work.

Those around us who are trying to heal from various "life wounds"—assault, life threatening illness, addiction—have encountered powerful forces rare in day-to-day living. This experience freezes ways of thinking and feeling at such basic levels that unspoken assumptions can be radically changed.

All of life can suddenly feel like a dark alley. Suddenly previous ideas about credible love, the balance of good and evil, and one's own safety are thrown horribly into doubt.

How we feel about being in the world is clearly reflected in our emotional "repertoire." As fear replaces joie de vivre, our emotional repertoire loses what I call its "roundness" and develops flat sides where some emotional expressions have been lost altogether. In working with trauma survivors, I ask them to look and see how "round" their emotional life seems to be.

One way to check for roundness is to use the "six healing sayings" I've been presenting to clients since 1982. It's an easy way to tell which feelings have been let out and which are still "shut-ins." These six sayings comprise all the really important messages one person gives another. I ask clients to ask themselves: "Which of these six messages are the easiest to say? The most frequently uttered? Which are the most difficult to say? Are there some which are never uttered? Does the pattern remain constant regardless of who you're with—family, co-workers, friends?"

The six sayings are the following:

1. "I love you."
2. "Thank you ."
3. "I'm sorry."
4. "I need help."
5. "That's not good enough."
6. " No! Stop! Bug off!"

Each of these is essential because they express feelings we cannot live without. The absence of any one of them denotes a numbness or starvation that deserves urgent attention.

"I love you"—in its most genuine form—is probably the most expansive of the six. It expresses joy, trust, power, and vulnerability all at once. The multiple realities expressed in this phrase contribute to the many forms of expression it takes. Someone who can't say "I love you"—or chooses not to—is, in a sense, standing at the edge of the river of life and suffering from thirst. This particular handicap can be the most painful to observe in oneself or in others, because the feeling is so essential.

"Thank you" is a statement of receiving and appreciation, and thus an acknowledgment of our interdependence. It is also a benchmark for those seeking a more spiritual life. Gratitude increases as fullness of "living in the light" increases. When "thank you" is missing, isolation reigns. This is particularly true in our culture, where ingratitude is perceived as arrogance and spreads ill feeling, whether at the kitchen table or in the boardroom. "Thank you" can be a very difficult phrase to say for people who have a chronic feeling that no matter what they receive, it isn't enough to make up for injustices suffered (such as sexual assault).

"I'm sorry" is our greatest expression of humility. It holds the overwhelming power of acknowledging and beginning to rectify injustice; it is our simplest and most exquisite example of nonviolent conflict resolution. Humility is powerful. It is often hard to understand that having power and being humble are not contradictory in nature.

"I need help" means asking that emotional needs be met. Oddly enough, reluctance to say this is often based not on a distaste for admitting need, and this is particularly true for those who have been abused as children-but on a fear that help is simply not available. A philosophy of scarcity has set in; there's an unspoken assumption that one is unworthy of receiving help or that there is simply not enough help to go around.

"That's not good enough" is a statement of power and need. It expresses self-worth and self-value; in its best sense, it brings everyone involved to attention. Saying "that's not good enough" is an ongoing work for people who are learning to fend off their own victimization. That's why it is so frequently heard in the AIDS epidemic. Having one's life threatened by not only disease but moral and legal condemnation as well has broken many lives. But it has also created some fierce warriors who cry, "That's not good enough!" and refuse to accept the terrible rumor that they are not entitled to society's compassion.

"No! Stop! Bug off!" is even more colorfully expressed in my workshops. The point is to make space, particularly recognized boundaries, and to express anger. Many people have been hurt by anger and equate it with violence. Quakers to some extent perpetuate the concept that anger can't be expressed without violence. Yet, honest anger and abuse are quite distinct. Shrieking "How dare you!" is not the same thing as striking a blow.

It is important to separate the two and to release the power of anger. Fury and indignation have saved many lives. People do not die from anger. But it may be that they die from stifling it. Inability to express anger has been documented as a contributing factor to cancer, heart attack, and depression. It can be a difficult thing to say because - like "I love you" — it is tremendously powerful. Unlike "I love you," it is not given enough cultural space to have its own natural rhythm and enter the waves of all feelings.

Want to start using one or more of these phrases more often? I suggest two things: being playful and paying close attention. Choose the three most important people in your life and recall a moment when you conveyed each of these sayings to them.

Or try this approach: Put your name in the middle of a blank page in your journal. Put the names of people important to you around the edge of the page. Recall your messages to each and mark them in one color. With another color, note their messages to you. With a third color write down the messages you would like to give or receive.

If you get a chance, work on this exercise with someone else who is also eager to expand. Have a dinner where you try to use all six sayings with one another: "Mom, please pass the peas and bug off." "Certainly, dear, and that's not good enough."

It sounds silly, but the stretch that one has to make to use these six sayings is one of the most elemental moves possible to counter the tendency to contract that comes after a traumatic experience. The reach to say what is felt has to be an expansive gesture. It opposes the natural tendency of the wounded to shut down. It is a determined reach for clarity.

A Ministry of Touch

August 1991

December 1983 - In October I had begun to research and organize getting massage to people with AIDS. I have found that I can do massage and not get AIDS, though no one seems to know how this disease works. Through the· Colorado AIDS Project and the Department of Health I began to give massage to a small group of men. It was quite a shock to enter into the lives of some of these people. It's as though leprosy has come back, the way some families, friends, and professionals act. For some, it changes their bodies so much they dare not go out in public. Some look as healthy as anyone else, but it can be seen in their eyes that the last kiss they had on the lips was 1-1/2 years ago.

August 1984 - My work this week is to help Mikel deal with his approaching death with the same grace he used to deal with his life—also, to deal with the fact that his caregivers are tired of giving to him. With Scott we are working on helping him maintain some sense of personal power while sight in his right eye leaves. For Ron we work on his recent realization that he is personally undernourished by an old pattern of giving, when he really wants to receive, which he is not good at. Last week he gave up some guilt about his father, and his whole face changed. Then he nervously asked to be held and cried a bit. He couldn't remember the last time he'd been held.

November 1984 - I am just completing one year of this work. Tomorrow I will pack my massage table, linens, and oils and drive to Denver to work with a man diagnosed last year with AIDS. When we began working together in June he had begun a decline. He is investing a good deal of energy denying this decline, and this has left him sleepless. Using a very carefully paced massage, I am able to help him move to a subconscious realization of his condition from his solar plexus. He begins to grieve his own life and then comes to see he could attend to his death with the same grace he used for his life.

February 1986 - From the audience of 100 men, a beautiful black man raises his hand and asks if there is any suspicion that the AIDS epidemic was planned. "Do any rich folks have it?" In a voice a bit black and faggy I say, “Well, you know Rock Hudson didn’t live downtown.” They all laugh very loud. For the first time I am in a prison teaching about AIDS. Their laughter is good and rids me of the doubt I had about reaching them. They’ve been wanting to know about AIDS since an inmate died last summer and another last week. In the last month the clinic has overflowed into the psychiatric ward with inmates who have AIDS. The sheets from the last deathbed were burned unwashed in a field. The men are scared, and the news I have to offer them is painful. By sharing needles they have been at risk for a few years now. They may have the virus. They may have already passed it to a wife and perhaps a child-to-be. I am as tender and clear as I can be. It is a painful witness.

October 1988 - I begin to see clients my second week back in DC. One fellow is very near dying, though he was quite hearty before I left. "Greg, what are you doing? You told me you were just going to stick around as long as it was fun." He replies, "Yes, well, my family is taking good care of me so I guess I am not ready yet." His family is in the next room, relieved that I am a professional they do not have to help. They do not want to watch. They do not touch him. They wash whenever they touch something he has touched. It is clear they love him deeply but in this setting they don't know how. The cancer has so disfigured him and made his breathing so difficult that not holding him or touching his hand hurts them nearly as much as the idea of doing so. They are very jealous of the nurse, the friend, the former lover, and me, because we touch in love and without fear. And for this the family finds something wrong with each of us.

December 1989 - I have been with Keith two weeks. Last night he asked me for massage and asked me what I felt. Oh, dear. So I tell him gently and clearly that I feel there is less of him each time we have worked over the last two years, less body and physical energy and always lots of spiritual energy. He says he's been wondering if he's dying. We share many ideas about this. He's certain he'll pass over easily at the right time and not commit suicide. He feels as though he's done his life's work and in that sense is ready to go, but simply doesn't want to go yet. He feels himself getting lighter, as though getting ready to fly away. He sees afterlife as a relief. I say I'd rather have him here, but only if it's fun for him, and I don't want him to wait until it's awful and leave in a huff without saying goodbye. I want him to watch and see when it's coming and do what's needed to make it a going-away party. . He laughs at this. He's so good. It's an honor to be asked to listen to the wanderings of this tender child who will be 37 on Christmas.

March 1991 - Last fall I helped half a dozen friends with AIDS to die. After seven years of this work I am both amazed and weary at the beauty and horror of this epidemic. I feel great joy in being of help. Two of the people I helped in the fall were lovers. Joe and Julio died within a few months of each other. Julio was from El Salvador and had helped the rebel army as a teenager. When I saw him last he was lying in his hospital room in great pain. He asked me why something so painful as the epidemic had come to gay people. "Why did God do this? We are not bad!" I held him and tried to ease the terror. "I don't know if there is reason or logic to this," I said, "but if there is, maybe God wants to show what happens when tender people are put into hard places." He liked that a lot. He died not long afterward. Joe was in another hospital and could not go to his memorial, which hurt very much.

February 1991 - The music is not very good. It is too white. It has the passion of white people "getting down." It is white bread fresh out of its plastic. To my right sits an old friend, someone I have loved for years. We know each other more and better than is comfortable, and this is precious. He has just found out he has the HIV infection, and he moves from laughter to fearful tears many times a day. The chorus leans into a song about AIDS. It is not a good song. It is schmaltzy and slow and needs a few beers to be thought beautiful. But the sentiment touches off a flood of tears in my friend. His body shakes silently. He hears them singing about him and about all our friends who've died. And who would be next? We are surrounded with many other people we know. They must not see this crying, because his positive test for the virus and his recent illness are not public. For now, they are secrets for the treasured few. I want to hold him as I did earlier in the day, but that would burst a dam of secrecy and restraint. I move my leg next to his and connect from knee to ankle. The man next to him is also sobbing. He is another friend of ours who also has the virus. He has just been told he should start toxic medications next week. He is terrified and bitter. They have a muted communion as the song wails on, feeling their fear with each other. They have traveled from two coasts to tell each other the same news. I feel my love for them. I am so fed up with AIDS. This moment of great fire has burned all its wood for now.

March 1991—Claude calls with great news. After ten years with AIDS and a roller coaster ride of near death and good health, he is being used to test a new medication. The initial test looks very good. There is no toxicity, and the drug does only what it was designed to do - to bond with the virus so that it cannot reproduce. His energy is better, and some infections are clearing. It makes us both teary. Dare we believe that the horrible can be made manageable?

Released to Do Good Works

November 1994

[Author's note – I was a Released Friend for 15 years from 1987 to 2002. It was an invaluable experience of learning and communication in spiritual community.]

In Minneapolis in 1988, I was teaching a seminar at the first national conference on massage for people with AIDS. I was not at all sure about my topic. Doubts abounded as the first speaker finished up and I took my place at the microphone. I had wanted to teach massage or my anti-burnout workshop, but I had contacted the organizers too late and they had those bases covered. Also they had never heard of me. "Could you teach fundraising?" they asked.

So, there I was explaining two ideas. First, there's a concept slowly being revealed out of the pain and injustices of the 20th Century, which is this: there is a level at which evil—such as apartheid, nuclear power, etc.—is no longer economically feasible. Conversely, goodness, defined as sharing wealth and working for the common good, has not yet shown an upper limit. As the tides turn ever so slowly, more money comes available for good works. Second, the way you raise money is to go out and do something beautiful and then say, "Who will help me?"

Well, they loved it. They even used these ideas to fund the following year's conference. There were a few skeptics who said, "How do you know these things?" to which I replied, "I'm a released Friend."

What is this Friends' tradition, and what mechanics are used? I want to share a few thoughts on this because it is a good and valuable tradition that should be preserved. I confess at the outset that my view is from an extreme experience: For over ten years I have lived primarily on gifts while following a leading to teach about healing from trauma.

I remember when I first heard the term. I had just spent two years asking friends for donations so I could continue to eat and pay rent while giving massage to people with AIDS for little or no pay. A good friend mentioned that it might be helpful if my Monthly Meeting "released" me.

"Is that like being set loose, Lyle?"

"In a way." he said.

With some more research I learned this wonderful and very old tradition in the Religious Society of Friends is used to help people follow a leading. The tradition goes something like this. A Friend received a leading to do good works and seeks clearness with his or her monthly meeting. The meeting will consider whether the leading is a genuine one, if the Friend is appropriate to the task, and if the task is a shared concern in the Meeting. If so, the Friend is supported in some way to help accomplish the work. That's the shell of the tradition. All of the particulars are the invention of each Meeting. It can be as simple as providing gas money for the Friend to go and talk to other meetings in the quarter about an issue of some importance. It can also be as complex as supporting a life's work.

For instance, Friend Obadiah might want to travel to a troubled place and make some sort of contribution of himself. The meeting considers the situation carefully. If they perceive that his work will be an extension of the meeting, and that it rightly will be done by him, they ask what he may need that they can give. Since he would be set apart from regular community life, would he need a good pair of boots, perhaps, or letters of introduction or relief from his milking chores. Will he need forgiveness from his monetary contribution to the meeting or his commitment to start up the wood stove in the meetinghouse early on First Days? Through this kind of searching together, early Friends sent out many people from their meeting to do things that one person had a passion for and all agreed needed doing.

Like many Quaker traditions, the spirit is the essence of the form, divine inspiration is its basis, and the external details are minimal. The first task of a meeting is to seek clarity about whether a Friend's leading is genuine. This can be difficult for Friends to sense, particularly if the individual is not yet active in a certain work. It is important that a meeting distinguish between passion that has muscle and idealism that may lose stamina in difficult times. There is also the problem of eccentricity, a quality that we Quakers adore in some and disdain in others. It is not your regular kind of person who takes on prison reform—not in 1794, and not now. This can make discerning a Friend's leading difficult. Spiritual seeking in its active stages can cause people to be highly inarticulate and odd. It is the essence of a person that must be sought to determine the genuineness of their leading. Depending on the leading, the Meeting will want the Friend to be genuine—crazy enough to do the work, but not too crazy.

The next task is to consider the Meeting's interest in the work—to measure its enthusiasm. It needn't be work that the meeting is excited about, since the first responsibility is to help the Friend seek.

The meeting must then consider what is needed and what can be offered or invented to help. Often, more will be needed than the meeting can give. This reflects the tension inherent in seeking and not the failure of the meeting as parent. The meeting is not a job bank or a panacea for every seeker who can't bear the suspense of how and when way will open. It also should be clearly understood by all that one need not to suffer in order to do good works. There is enough to do without having to worry that a great deal of work may collapse because the phone has been turned off. As we support people who are good at giving, we much be watchful for unnecessary sacrificing of their own basic needs to give more to others.

Discerning the essence of a leading and nurturing it for good health, or helping to bring it into maturity, is the responsibility of the meeting. The primary task of doing one's best work and being faithful to a leading belongs to the seeker, who should bear in mind that directions change and broaden as time goes on. Leadings change with the maturing ability to listen without hearing one's own wishes. The true test of a mature ministry is that the tone of one's best reverent work is absorbed and exuded in one's everyday living. Speaking well at Meeting does not excuse one's rudeness anywhere else in life.

The release is recognition that spiritual questing involves doing good works. This must also be understood for what it is and what it is not. We do good works to reform our interior, to seek, learn, change, and come closer, if only for moments, to the Divine. The fact that it will be of help to others in direct ways is merely good design on the part of the universe. The difficulties of doubt, fatigue, and losing finite ideas of purpose are not flukes; they are to be expected. More often, way opening resembles a shooting star rather than the yellow brick road. It is a journey not merely a ride. No one is honored by ongoing suffering, however, so love of work and joy must be kept track of deliberately.

Since release can be the essence of spiritual life one can assume that language will be insufficient to express what is witnessed. We must strive to say somehow what we saw, felt, and heard, but we can also anticipate some frustrations. Once we begin to put words to describe spiritual experience, we dilute it. It can help the meeting to trust that all love and good work go to the common good. Sensing and feeding the effort, not policing it, is the meeting's boundary. The released seeker should understand that the work itself is one's road and home for the period of release.

My Meeting in Putney, Vermont, has two released Friends. Eva Mondon began working as a massage therapist. She has devoted her life to helping people who are healing from suffering. As massage fell away from her practice, her leading included breath work, imagery, drums, and always prayer. Her understanding of what she does moved from massage therapist to Quaker Witness for Healing. Her release and mine happened about the same time and have similar structure. We both have Minutes naming the nature of our leadings, describing the meeting's appreciation and support of our work. To bring renewal and reassessment into the structure, there is a three-year limit to the Minute. We are not in the meeting's budget; the meeting established a contributory fund whereby individuals or other meetings can donate anonymously as they are led. (Anonymity is a lovely thing. Remember, the only thing our Society shies away from talking about more than sex is money!)

Both Eva Mondon and I have oversight committees to help us, as needed, seek clarity—and to offer other support. One member of my committee takes care of thank-you notes to donors whose names and addresses are passed on by the treasurer. This is good for anonymity and a true blessing for anyone with a desk like mine that seems to sneeze out too many letters to be answered. Both Eva and I have presented our work in various ways to the meeting. Eva is a member of Thich Nhat Hanh's Tiep Hien Order, which stresses mindfulness. She is generous with her Buddhist candles and uses a healing quilt made for her work by the meeting. I keep a journal at the meetinghouse, which includes various writings and my calendar. I add to this every so often.

Things should be kept as simple and neighborly as possible. Release should increase a sense of reverence about good work and a Meeting's sense of its generosity. If that is not there, I would wonder why.

The released Friend tradition is one that helps us support the still small voice within. Does a meeting have more spiritual life going on than is given voice? Is there work that needs doing that we are not sure how to touch? Can we give the space Spirit needs within us? What do you support now that reflects your inner knowing?

I think of the essence of release as having two levels, really. One is that the involvement of the meeting acts as a cultural base, a firm ground from which one extends outward. But the true nature of release is this: If you truly feel you are doing what you are supposed to, you will come to know and expect that way will open; common fears will be laid down, and you will be allowed to know your life outside the worldly definitions that keep us huddled and confused in this noisy world and outside spiritual life.

When I took the leap I had faith that I would find a net, instead I learned I could fly.

True Love

February 1994

Dear Loved Ones,

I am sending this letter to both of you. You don't know each other, and you are from different parts of the country with no reason to meet. One of you has lost a love and is hungry for another. One of you has found a love without looking and is terrified. Both of you have told me what you're feeling and wonder what to do next. I am sitting here late at night with Marshall asleep beside me and thinking how amazing, threatening, wonderful, and scary is this bizarre thing of true love, of a partner, of the task of giving and receiving intimacy. I am also wondering how I got here, where I am with my love, and what I know about this. I feel like I don't know much, at least not for sure, but I want to try to make a few notes and see what comes out. Actually I think very little is known about how partners/spouses/lovers work, especially finding them, and that may be the most true thing I know.

First off, I don't think anyone really understands how you get a turn at having a true love. Nobody. Some folks say you gotta be out there circulating and letting the world know you're in the market. But I was in the market for a long time.

What did I find? More men than Bob Hope saw in Viet Nam, but no true love—never. I know some folks have been out there longer than I have, sipping from every fountain and still thirsty. I also know folks who didn't even have to wait long, weren't looking and BOOM– first try—true love and long lasting. How come? If I knew I would be flying us all to Paris for the weekend right now. Some folks get great turns at love. Some folks get lousy turns. Some folks get one turn. Some folks get lots. And I know some folks who get none. So how does it work? Nobody knows.

I remember sometime back in June of 86, I was moaning and griping, "Oh I got no lover! Woe is me! Life is hard enough without being lonely too. Plus, I ain't getting any younger and I wasn't that marketable to start with." So I had a talk with God and I said, "So, this is my life? No partner? Just dear friends and a life's work of helping people and no one special? Is that really what you have in mind for me? Fine, I accept but you gotta send more money!" And that's when I gave up. I knew I was very confused about the difference between being in bed and being in love. I knew I had a history of short term things I thought were love but weren't.

So, what did I have to lose by giving up? Only my confusion. And my painful longing. And being angry at people who barely knew me for not falling in love back. Oh dear, how tacky. A graduate degree in confusion. For years I attached every hurt and disappointment I had ever had to these near misses, and that summer, when I was 34, I'd had enough. Enough trouble, enough hurt, and enough not knowing how it worked.

Then one day when I wasn't looking, here comes Marshall just as sweet as you please on the last warm day of summer at the gay swimming hole. He'd never been there. After a couple of dates I knew this was the real thing. I knew cause it scared the bejesus out of me. I realized that I was going have to surrender all the obstacles I usually put in the way and this made me so scared I cried all day.

What did I learn from this? Two things, I think. One—it's like looking for shooting stars. The best way to do it is you go out in a field at night, lie down, and you don't look anywhere in particular, just up. No focusing on one place. Just taking in the whole sky in general and relaxing. Sort of like saying, "I've been making a life for myself that I want to live and it's a pretty good design in progress and maybe I'm going to see some shooting stars tonight and maybe not. And maybe the light that my life shines will draw a light toward me."

Two—surrender to love is the hardest damn work I have ever done in my life. I can help tortured women who haven't slept without nightmares in ten years to relax. I can work in prisons to teach murdering rapists how to give a good massage, but don't ask me to be open and receive the tender loving care of someone who is going to know all my dirty laundry and stick around anyway!

Why is that so hard? Well, I guess I have just been on the road so long I don't know the difference between my feet and my boots. Then here comes someone to offer a foot rub, and I gotta feel how tired my feet are and how long I've been wanting to be touched. I gotta lay down all those other times of disappointment and confusion and let this in without overwhelming myself or anyone else with grief and longing. I didn't learn how to do this at home or school. Did you? It takes a combination of mercy that we give to ourselves. Did you ever know how to do that?

I also know this, though I have to remind myself—loneliness is mean. Not getting the hugs and kisses we all need makes us sick and crazed, and do all kinds of things we don't want to talk about. We look in places we shouldn't, and we go on about other people's business so we don't have to feel our own burden, and we get too busy to feel. Now, after seven and a half years of being with Marshall, I have to think back for a moment to remember how it was not knowing where that next hug or kiss was going to come from and how that made me feel ugly, dumb, poor, crippled, and some days worse than that.

I think being lonely is a special kind of pain. Maybe it's one we know well and even get use to. I think it takes a special kind of caring for ourselves to love and embrace that lonely part of us, to kiss that hurt and bring it out into the light so it doesn't fester into some worse monster than it is. To bare that scarred place and give it some special cream and massage, to know it and own it and feel it. Not to define all our being, but to acknowledge this part of us and love it. I think this makes it the least heavy it can be.

I also think that to have a partner is the hardest ongoing work in the world. As they say, "There is no easy chair of love." I remember the story about the German shepherd who went running down the road chasing after the Volkswagen. Well, he caught it and thought, " Now what do I do?"

I don't think I have ever worked so hard in my life as I have trying to make a good marriage, which I think means the horrible task of unfolding into our best selves, peeling off the old, unusable layers of all that has been gathered and learned over the years that does not honor our best selves. And always there is more to do. There's a wonderful saying in the Talmud: "You don't have to finish this task, but you can't lay it down either."

A few principles come to mind. You have to live together or you'll only scratch the surface of what it can be. You have to believe that it's forever or you'll never really unpack and reveal your essence. You can't jump in the water and then yell about getting all wet.

One of the ways I watch to see how we are doing is to notice the joy or delight level as it moves. I think it should bounce a bit, move but not ricochet too much. I also think it's a good sign when we are both spending time each week adoring each other and also wondering to ourselves, "How does he put up with me?" A friend observed this about us- "I can tell it's a good marriage because one of you will say "It's this way." and the other one says, "No it's not. It's this way." And the first one says, "Really?" So I can tell you don't have too much investment in reality." (Which we all know is highly overrated.)

Something that has been a real shock for me is that I had no idea how deeply I would feel protective of someone else's feelings. On the list of things mother never told me goes the whole concept that when you are partners, a part of you is out there in the world that you cannot protect and this will break your heart whenever there is danger or even the suggestion of danger. Even though I have spent a lifetime learning, using, and teaching healing, when someone is mean to my man I turn into the Wicked Witch of the West. It is not pretty or logical, or desirable and has got me in trouble on more that one occasion. But I become full bloom Mafia avenger when someone hurts him. I still wonder at this. It's not OK. It is homework I did not expect.

Another shock is that there always seems to be enough love to deal with even the most enormous hurt or conflict between us. We have tested this reluctantly, unintentionally, and found, to our great relief, that life apart is out of the question. The question is always—what are we going to do with this obstacle? And like all other traumas, if we can use it for learning, then we can turn pain into wisdom. But it means doing the homework—reaching, changing, and going to new ground without maps.

Sometimes I wonder if this is why so many marriages fail. Where in life do we have any preparation to be shown our worst selves by someone who loves us and understand it as a gift to become better at being who we are? Have we ever learned to love this even from the graceful parent or the talented teacher?

Now it is much later than when I began this wondering, on beyond midnight. The winter sky is clear and bright with stars and the moon. The wind comes now and again to ring the chimes outside the window. I will read this over tomorrow, but I think what little I know about the finding of true love and the work of partnering is all here. I send it as a blessing with much love, John

Having a Gift

July 1999

Having a gift is often thought to be a small blessing. In my very large Italian family various individuals were recognized informally for their gifts in ways that said, this is a small blessing and it puts you ahead, not apart, in this one category. It was known that Uncle Nick had "the gift of gab," a way with a story and a tone of voice that would draw people to listen. He used this as an announcer at county fairs. Cousin Ro had a gift for compassion in teaching. The most difficult children, who would drive other adults around the bend, would trust and respect her requests for hard work and cooperation. She's a master teacher by example and profession. My mother's mother had a sense of moral order that held her eleven children and thirty grandchildren in a very particular expectation of behavior and attitude. This stood everyone in good stead when in not so many years apart the farmhouse burnt down, her husband died, and World War II took her sons away to fight. Chaos was held at bay by her gift to know, and to keep before everyone, what was important.

In every grouping of people, some individuals are thought of being particularly good at this or that. In a village or congregation or organization, it's common that for a time, sometimes in cycles, certain needs are met by certain people who have a knack. An anthropologist friend says that a group of up to 100 is a good size for everyone to know everyone. It's in this small setting that gifts become known and used. Of course, many things can be learned and it's important that everyone not do just what they knew yesterday or stick to specialties. And yet there is a comfort for a group in seeing a task done by ones who have a gift for it, a comfort we sometimes lose by structure.

All gifts call for learning: balance, envy, humility, reverence, awareness, sorting out various parts, and the uses of power, etc. These tests of knowledge are not the problem with having a gift but simply part of the whole. If you have a gift and you learn it well, it's light and the gift you can offer, is brighter. If you don't learn about this gift, and hence yourself, then there are some wonderful colors that are not going to be seen by you or others. My Uncle John had a gift for languages. He taught himself four of them. But he was in a family that strove to Americanize quickly, so only his gift with English was admired.

When a gift has a particular significance in one's world, then it becomes more than a small blessing. When the gift is overtly spiritual, the learning necessary to use it well is more extensive. And its meaning in one's life will have more consequence.

I have been talking with friends over the years about the condition of having a gift, its delight and its burdens. These are not easy conversations, in part because one is taught to eschew discussing one's better parts so as not to indulge in vanity. And in truth, if one is going to sit around sipping iced tea and bragging about all one has done so very well, then vanity, not study, is accomplished, and this is perfectly boring. But to focus on having a gift for the task of doing God's will or giving to the common good or bringing one's spiritual life continually into the current moment—this is excellent work and we should encourage it.

I have repeatedly considered the burdens of having a gift. There is always the issue of power, which is revealed in many, many ways. Who has it? What kind is it? What are they doing with it? How did they get it? And what does that mean for everyone else? The more power one's gift has, the more care, reverence, and stillness (perhaps slowness) one needs to exercise. This was very clear to me as a teacher of young children a quarter of a century ago. A teacher has great power, sometimes too great a power, and it must be expressed deliberately and consciously so as not to inhibit or harm anyone.

Having a gift that has obvious power will always make someone nervous, and for good reason. Power, not well studied, has been a source of great pain and confusion throughout the history of humankind. But sometimes our culture skews this to teach that we are all equal and, since there is that of God in everyone, we are all the same. Our push for diversity can sometimes be inarticulate and suggest that we really are all the same although in seemingly different packages. This is not as clear as it could be. We want to be careful to find ways to acknowledge difference, especially where a child's gifts and power are concerned, so that spiritual blossoming in a decidedly unspiritual world has a hand up. The mark of mature use of having a gift with power can often be seen in the grace one does or doesn't know to use with this gift.

Having a gift seems to be, in general, information that comes to one from elsewhere. One may even be engaged in working the gift, expressing it clearly in some way, but be unaware of it. We don't declare it or wish it or write a grant for it or receive it by longing. Somehow we get told that something seems to grow more easily in us. This telling can come from those we serve or those who know to watch for such things (another skill that old Quakers go unrecognized for) or from sources unexpected or unfamiliar. The seeds of having a gift seem to have inklings early in life for some but maybe not enough to be obvious until one looks back on the journey.

Having a gift always has consequences to it. It will mean responsibility that one should not try to dodge. It will always mean learning and failure and more learning without end. And those of us who are reluctant students have to come round to loving the hard work of sorting out what we can't see. The suspense alone is something I have the least patience with.

As others recognize or don't recognize one's gift, forces to pull one forward and obstacles to hold one back will rise up, shift, and fade. And what seems to be help and what seems to be hindrance may not be clear. One doesn't push way open, after all. And what may appear to be a wall today may reveal itself as a seat belt tomorrow.

Having a gift is not for sissies, but for the brave of heart. Nor is it for saints. A wonderful old Quaker woman renowned for her good works had many saintly stories told at her memorial meeting some years ago. But the pithier stories of great strength and not a little vulgarity told later over brandy showed she also had an a ability to be as diverse as needed.

Being faithful means more then asking what God requires. There is also being faithful to one's self-knowledge, one's sense of proportion and limits, and stretching beyond what one knows. Often discernment will have many pieces that either refuse to hold still for us or seem oppositional. How often we come to learn that opposites are actually good friends. And how often the limits of our own literal interpretation block the vision given us. There is also the quality of being not too specific. If we try to be too particular in seeking understanding of having a gift, we may miss the broad scope a gift may offer. We may frustrate ourselves by asking for a job description when what we really need to learn next is a change of tone.

Having a gift can be a burden depending on the gift itself and who has it. I know one friend who is called to preach. Which is all well and good except that she is shy to the point of illness with each new opportunity to preach. For her, the hard part is not the preaching. She's learned to surrender in order to receive that. But the irrational fear of public speaking even after years of success makes each work an act of faith and endurance.

Another friend is called to teach about spiritual life and particularly seeking the Holy Spirit each moment. He is called to do this by talking about his own life, which is all well and good, except that his life has been terribly messy. Again the preaching has gone fine. He's learned to trust his guidance. But he's horribly embarrassed to be using his life as a "don't do it this way" example. It's been a mandatory graduate degree in humility he never intended and his work is sterling.

Another friend has the gift to know when heart bypass surgery is needed immediately. She may meet up with someone in the middle of the day at the grocery store, feels the reality of their heart disease in her own chest, and then must find some way to get this person to the doctors for tests now without scaring them or having them think she's nuts. Her gift for theater has also increased dramatically.

Another friend, who is blind, can see the colors surrounding someone's body and thereby know whether the illness or discomfort they feel is emotionally based or actually in the physical body as disease. One can only imagine the obstacles to this gift living in a science-based culture.

I have struggled with many similar troubles over the years. I declared my gift was exactly X when I was still learning its scope thus limiting myself. I insisted that it was a constant condition without admitting my own inconstant disciplines to be faithful and thus denied myself the hope of getting better at it. I have claimed righteous indignation as a natural result without owning my need for further work on old anger.

I currently struggle with two pieces in particular. The gift I have is a particularly intimate one. I learn stories of pain. Sometimes the gift of releasing pain, which of course comes not from me but through me, makes me seem like an old friend. But really we just met for the afternoon workshop. In a worldly way, we really don't know each other at all. And what I have learned of their pain, I have to release and clear to make space to help another. And this might happen to me hundreds of times a year. It's intimacy on a grand scale. It can mean misunderstandings, sometimes painful, of who we are to each other.

Another struggle is to sort out the differences for me in certainty and arrogance. Since my gift is mainly for the wounded and their caregivers, I tend to tread where there is much pain. The certainty I am given when I am lead to work on someone can be a welcomed oasis for the chronically fearful. There's nothing quite like someone's confidence about where shore lies when the boat seems to be sinking. But when ego, fatigue, fear, or all three converge in my responses, I can be as graceless as anyone in spite of an amazing gift. It's not a contradiction so much as a vigil to keep learning and owning the grace and the grouch—with equal humor, humility, and reverence.

I am also continually shocked at how retractable and illusive a state of grace can be. It's not uncommon for me to awake in a thoroughly angry nightmare-fed condition, practice my spiritual disciplines, and do beautiful work at mid-day. And by evening slide back into some more unattractive aspect of a self that flees the light. I think there has been improvement over the years and am confirmed of this by dear friends, but the trip over the line is always a mystery and a disappointment. Becoming a grace junkie is part of learning the disciplines of surrender to Spirit. Letting it in and letting it go, being grateful for having been chosen and used rather than missing its absence.

Learning one's gift is a life long work. Since my surrender to this gift in the early 1980s, there are many pieces I have learned and feel to be routine. But oddly enough this doesn't seem to have diminished the number or intensity of the parts I have yet to understand. Often the learning in spiritual work comes after the steps are taken and one pauses to look back, and then wonders about the next steps.

The benefits of having a gift are enormous. I feel as though I have a union contract for life. Each time I ask about the terms of my lease, I get very clear responses that I have only recently been put into any decent refurbished shape and there's lots to do and no end of work in sight any time soon. I am assured that my grades on the surprise quizzes could be better, but there seems to be greater patience for me at headquarters then I have for myself. More learning about learning. It also confirms for me my experience of being different. This is a comfort as opposed to feeling strange for no reason.

When one seeks to see where the beginning was, the clues may come slowly. I know one friend was told of his gift in high school by a passing stranger. I know another gift came to a friend in early childhood and she didn't speak of it for decades. There are ways our culture keeps us in the dark about our own spiritual autobiographies. Do we know our own paths well enough to tell our stories from several perspectives? It's true that I left being a school teacher and went to massage school because I wanted to help at a deeper level. It's also true I planned to work on cruise ships, spa work not being known for its depth. It's also true that when my cousins and I fell into a patch of nettles on my grandmother's farm, I led everyone down to the brook where I made mud packs and then administered the sap of a weed to relieve the sting. I was five years old.

I have a friend who is a wonderful writer. His glimpses into human mystery amaze. He body is twisted. His speech is unclear. He's strapped into a wheelchair. For others to know his gift, he must either be published or we must reach out into his life seeking his light. It's been more than worth the trip for me to reach and learn who's behind the initial impression so full of my own bias. How many people are there whose gifts are not served by our culture's meager help to grow in this way? Do we know the difference of not seeing and not looking and the ways our structures maintain the blind spots?

Seeking and Shoveling

October 2003

I have been devoted to a spiritual discipline lately whose lessons I believe may help us to bear with some of the difficulties in discussing the important tasks of social change and civil rights. The discipline I'm involved in, of taking the worst from the dark and bringing it out into the light for the miracle of growth, might teach us much. I speak, of course, of shoveling out the outhouse. I want to relate this task to the great Quaker tradition of seeking, and especially seeking around controversy and conflict. There are several common parts and principles that can help us. I offer them here to encourage us all to continue to share deeply and honestly.

THIS IS LIFE OUT OF THE ORDINARY

This shoveling task is not reasonable. I have an image of summer being spent at a swimming hole, of sipping iced tea, even of bringing in hay on a bright sunny day from open fields of great light. So, to take a shovel and go into a cavern never meant to be stood in is quite out of the ordinary, not regular life.

Thus it is with seeking, especially where there is any pain, urgency, or intimacy. And because it's out of the ordinary we can expect to bump into things and move without grace at times. This doesn't mean we should turn back. It means we should go carefully, and remember how to say, "I don't know what this means" when that is our condition. We can all expect surprises that will make us uncomfortable, whether it's seeing what we don't understand or having to say what we don't want to say. Just know, as in The Wizard of Oz, that we are not in Kansas anymore and that's partly why we are seeking.

THE TASK IS LONG

I take off the outdoor panel on the low part of our house's slope and there, filling the doorway and overflowing its way into my heart, sinuses, and sneakers, is a mixture of poop and peat moss. I take a very large shovel, like the one my Uncle John used after every milking to clean the barn, and I fill a small garden cart with four shovelfuls. Then I have to push the cart up a little hill, past the vegetable bed with its growing population of snakes, and then a bit more uphill to where my husband,

Marshall Brewer, has dug a long trench for the new iris bed. It will take four days and over 100 trips to do this.

Likewise, to sort out, hear deeply, speak honestly, and accommodate all the discomfort with this topic will not take a short time. It will take many, many trips back and forth. So let's pace ourselves for the long haul. Community is worth the time and care.

THE TASK IS MOST SPECIFIC

Moving something that has needed to rest in the dark until it's ready, and bringing it out into the light and putting it in the right place to plant something wonderful whose shape and color will delight us all could upset some folks in a big way. Simply asking a question is making trouble—good Godly trouble, a fine old Quaker tradition. Can we keep our eyes on the intention and off the we/they, win/lose traps that lie all around us? If we can't, it doesn't spell failure. It probably means there is more pain than we can hold and still move right now.

I AM NOT WELL-SUITED TO THE TASK

Though I am less bothered than many by the disgusting parts of shoveling out a compost toilet, it would be better if I had heavy eyebrows to direct the sweat away from my eyes. And though I am strong, it would be better if I were not carrying so much extra weight before lifting the shovel. So, too, is the question for each of us: what do I bring to this process that may not help bring it to clarity? Can I declare this lack of clarity honestly?

ALL PROGRESS COMES FROM UNREASONABLE PEOPLE

If you are seeking the spiritual nature of a particular situation or clarity as to the how and why of a thing, you can expect trouble, and delightfully so. When Margaret Fell said, "We'll have to go into that prison and shine God's love upon them," do you think for one moment everybody answered, "Sure, Meg, I'll pack the picnic baskets." Heck, no. They were thinking, "How can I get out of here and how did this woman get the keys to everything with her lunatic dreams?" When we act out to ask the hard questions and suggest that there needs to be a change, we should expect that not everything is going to be light and fluffy, or go quickly, or be acceptable dinner conversation.

I can recall doing my first AIDS education in a prison in 1985. No reasonable person should have been allowed to attempt it. It called for a combination of theater, social work, and science that no school teaches. It reminds me of our dearly departed wonderful Quaker peace teacher Bill Kreidler's important Peaceable Kingdom talk, where he asks us to be grateful in prayer for the conflict in our lives. While I understand Bill's idea, in my imperfection the closest I can get is to say, "Thank you that today didn't hurt as much as it could have."

And so if we are involved in covering new territory, it would be good if we didn't take personally many of the things that might get aimed our way. Jumping in the water and then complaining about being wet is no way to accomplish social change at home or in the world. Anticipate the misunderstandings and the misinterpretations, and try not to be insulted by them. It's part of the work.

CAN WE TRULY WELCOME HONESTY AND PAIN?

Honesty and pain are necessary parts of the change of seeking. If you are desirous of change without honesty or pain you're better off sticking with television, where trouble has an 18-minute format. In real life all reform—from mental health institutions to a woman's role in the family to the decisions about new weapons—will involve hearing things that are so ignorant or so true as to be frightening. And we cannot do without any of these truths. They have to be brought out and given light and space for us all to see how the problem is stuck, how it is constructed, what part can be worked with now, and what part later. It's vital to ask for all the honesty, including the worst possible expressions, to come forth. It's in the light of each person's essence that we can see what exactly we have to work with and how it all fits together. As the brave drag queens of the Stonewall Rebellion knew, change is no place for sissies.

IS THE TIMING AND MOVEMENT ORGANIC?

Some work simply has to wait in the dark until it's ripe for change. Then comes the day when it's right to shovel and someone with a shovel shows up and the change begins. If it's not the right time, or there's no shovel, or the person is squeamish about what the shovel is touching, a long and difficult work can be made more so.

BE MINDFUL OF WEARINESS

There is that terrible kind of mid-term fatigue that says, "Whose idea was this anyway? I'm pooped. Let someone else change the world. I'm going home to sit with a brew and watch the ballgame." This is a good honest place to come to in difficult work. Anyone who doesn't know this pit stop of doubt and fatigue hasn't been on much of an adventure. It includes blaming the leadership and feeling guilty for not being or doing enough. It's known in every organization that's attempting large work. Let's make space for it and not freak out when it shows up, and let's give the person with doubt, fatigue, and pain a hug and a kiss and a break in the pace, and see if we can then go on together.

NO LOVE IS WASTED

Every act of compassion finds a home and goes where it's needed whether or not we can see where it lands. Most often, our task is to fashion our best love, give it our best delivery, bless it, and let it go. How it's received, where it goes, how it's used is beyond us, and often beyond where we can see. Let us trust our best efforts and surrender our self-doubt and uneasiness and desires for control to the Holy Spirit, knowing the part we played is smaller in the long view.

WE CANNOT HEAL WHAT WE FEAR

If there is something we want to bring to light it has to be something we are willing to witness, touch, and know. Anyone thinking that an important change can happen easily because it's a good idea needs some more time in a trench that nobody likes—such as the AIDS pandemic, or the crisis of rape or hunger and homelessness, or the common uses of violence to dominate in conflict. We will learn more, more than we want to learn, more than is comfortable, if we chose to seek deeply and honesty no matter what trouble we witness.

And, of course, that witness will change us forever. What we see and know stays with us. In the end, any monster, inward or outward, needs us to stop trying to kill it or being terrified of it, to gather up all possible grace and sit next to the monster for a nice cup of tea.

All of this is a great deal to ask, maybe too much to ask. Even with a large shovel and a strong back we will need time, patience, and endurance. A mature minister will have to make many trips no matter how short the walk. Listening inwardly and outwardly, sidestepping the various potholes, and placing the next stepping stone just before it's needed is more common in seeking and shoveling than we care to keep track of.

Working toward the common good, healing for ourselves and others, and working unknowns into understanding, change, and knowledge will always keep us in awe of so many moving pieces and, hopefully, grateful that we are never working alone.

Quakers, Sexuality, and Spirituality

Quaker Leadership Scholars Lecture, Guilford College

June 2004

Talking about sex in any context, even a Quaker one, can be dangerous because we don't all use the same language. We have different experiences. Sex holds different priorities in various people's lives. So, I just want to be clear that I am speaking only from my own experience. I am not speaking on behalf of gay men even though I am a member of that circle. I'm not speaking on behalf of first-generation Italian-American immigrants even though I am one. Or Quakers who know how to yodel. I'm just speaking from my own experience.

My own experience includes several different levels. On one level, I was raped and beaten as a young child, so I understand sex as a power to hurt. I am also someone who has spent the last 22 years giving massage and energy work to people who are recovering from traumatic experience. From this I understand the power of touch, sensuality, and intimacy to bring someone back to fullness, to bring someone back to the joy of life after perhaps thinking one could never love life again.

I'm also speaking to you as someone who is 50 years old and came out during that glorious, golden age of gay male sexuality after penicillin but before HIV. I want to tell you it was a good time to learn how to dance—to get out there and have some fun. During this time, gay male sexuality began to move from being sick and illegal toward being something that could be wonderful. It could be a delight. You could meet new people. You could even meet a future spouse at the gay swimming hole like I did.

Another part of my experience, after having a full dance card for several years, is that for 15 years I have been happily monogamous, which is a very different experience. I am talking from all these different perspectives.

I recently spoke with a Quaker sex educator, of which there are very few. When I asked Peggy Brick of New Jersey, "Are you the only one?" she said, "Well, actually Quakers have been very slow about sex education. Other churches have done a lot more than we have." There were some Quakers who had done sex education a few decades ago but she said they were mostly dead.

I've pretty much come to the conclusion that it's nearly impossible for Quakers to have sex. I'm sorry to inform you of this but it's true for a couple of different reasons.

One obstacle is the tradition of simplicity. There is a desire among Friends—a testimony, a witness—to keep life simple. Those who are going to fall in love or have an affair are going to mess up their simplicity. We are talking major trouble here. Are they going to call back? How does my hair look? And that's just the beginning. Wait until you're in the seventh year of a marriage and you realize you're still at the beginning! If you really want simplicity, if you're truly devoted to that as a witness, I recommend that you never have sex with anyone and that you never fall in love. It can't be done simply. It feels too wonderful. It feels too deeply.

There's another obstacle. This is, essentially, that Quakers don't like power. Quakers would prefer that no one have a lot of power. We would like to divvy it up so everyone has just a little bit and no one has a great deal of it. If you are looking to retire from the entire concept of power, sex is just not going to work because it's such a powerful force. It is such a large thing. It's such a wonderful power.

I had a friend named Mary. When she was almost 70 years old, she was tired and had arthritis and it was changing her body and she was hurting all the time. Well, Mary fell in love with a fellow who was about 22. They went into her bedroom, locked that door, and didn't come out until about three weeks later. Her arthritis was almost gone. She said, "I wish my doctors had explained this to me years ago." She was standing upright. She was smiling. The power of true love, the power of sexual attraction is huge. If power scares you, then there is going to be some difficulty. One of the lovely things about sexuality is to discover that power within yourself, to feel how lush it is, to feel how beautiful it is in someone else, and to join those things together. It's wonderful.

There's another problem with Quakers having sex. It is that there's a very strong, unspoken tradition among Quakers: you're not supposed to bring attention to yourself. Think about that time that you had a while ago—or maybe that you are looking forward to having—when you have been with that person who just melts your butter, who you look at and you think, "Ooh-la-la!" How wonderful. And you start to feel that tingling feeling and you say slowly, with a deep voice and heavy breath: "Darling, I just love what you're wearing tonight, and I just want to tell you I love you so much and I thank God we're together and I'm just wondering if you could come over here and be by me for a while." Now, if you don't want to call any attention to yourself, you have got to take that whole feeling and set it aside. You're going to sound like someone with a high, whiny voice, like, "Honey, would you mind if . . . oh no, no, it's not that important." With sexuality you want to love that power. You want to feel it. You want to know it in yourself. You want to find a way to work with it, live with it, and love it. That's very important.

Think what it would be like if we Quakers were more honest about our sexual lives. Think about some of our lovely elders after meeting on Sunday morning, coming out on the porch and saying, "Oh, thank God. Last night we made love! My whole body feels better. Thank God for giving me these feelings. I love my life more now. I like being in the world more. I can spend more time with the pain of the world now because I have felt its beauty deeply. Thank God! I can come home to my body and feel this wonderful inclusion." Isn't that great? But, if you can't call attention to yourself, that's going to be a problem.

There are some wonderful parallels between a spiritual life and a sexual life. These are parts of our lives that we do not always connect. We live in a very noisy world that in many ways is contrary to a deep spiritual life, working against it. This is especially so in U.S. culture. Popular culture is loud and tells everyone to go out and buy everything all the time.

In some ways, a sexual life is the same. There's such a noise in popular culture about what sexuality should be or could be, what with our being used to buying and selling things and people. In some ways we don't touch the deeper parts of either spirituality or sexuality unless we actually seek them out, wonder about them consciously, and try to learn about them within our own lives. If you look at the external details of people's sexual or spiritual lives, we all look very different. It's an incredible mosaic. But then if you look at the essential details on the inside, the needs of each of us, the longing that each person has, these essences are remarkably similar, both person to person and from sexuality into spirituality.

Another way in which there is a similarity between sexuality and spirituality is that it's sort of a big, blind date that everyone goes out on because we have this hunger within us. There's a desire and a hunger for grace, to feel that aspect of the Divine within ourselves—to feel some familiarity with a power greater than us. There is also that yearning for romance and for touch, just the right touch for us. It is highly individual and unique.

I was talking with a young, gay friend in Mexico. He had just gone out on a date and was wondering if it was true love or simply passionate fun. In describing it, he became sad. After talking about it for a while, he realized it really wasn't the sadness of what had happened on this date, but a sadness that can come because there is this great longing to stop looking. We all have a great hope that there is going to be true love: someone who we're not going to have to do a lot of translating with because they know all about us. This great longing within each of us is present in both the realm of the Divine and the realm of sex.

There's another parallel. This is hard to talk about because it's a concept that a lot of people are beat up with. It's the idea of sin. I'm thinking of sin as the things that take us away from the Divine, things that take us away from knowing spiritual life more deeply. The parallel for sexuality—I'm not sure this is the right word, but it's a word that can be used—is whoring. By that, I don't mean prostitution. I mean sex that takes you away from honoring yourself; sex that takes you away from feeling deeply, from beautiful intimacy; sex that takes you away from personal power. The interesting thing about the whoring of sex and the sin in spiritual life is that there is no part-time work. If you are signing up for one of those two destructive activities, it's full-time and it will take you away from your best self. But these concepts have to be applied individually because they are all going to mean different things in our individual lives and experiences. There isn't going to be someone to tell you the right way to have a life with God or have a life with sex. It is such intimate seeking that it has to be done individually, finding the right language to tell one another what we've seen and felt along the way.

I think the most important similarity between these two realms is the concept of surrender. By this, I don't mean giving up. We have aspects of ourselves that long for something larger and greater than us. If you learn how to surrender in one realm, you can transfer that wisdom into other realms. If you know about surrendering to true love, then there's the possibility that you can use that learning for surrender to deeper spiritual experience. If you have done the surrender to deeper spiritual experience, you can use that learning for surrendering to true love. The latter is never an easy surrender because life hurts so much. Sometimes true love comes along—if it does come along, and it sometimes seems we have been waiting a long time, too long—but when it does come along, you have to ask yourself: "Can I unpack the bags? Take out all my disappointments, all my anxiety, and set them aside and really join with this other person?"

This is true of romantic love, but it's also true of more casual relationships. There are lots of different kinds of surrender, lots of ways of learning about this very important concept. When we learn surrender in one place, we can use it to surrender in another place.

I want to conclude with a description. It is this: I take a very tender part of myself and relax it completely. I find that I am able to surrender to something larger than just me. There are many different and amazing feelings and lots of sensation. It can become very exciting and exhausting. It concludes, I experience separation, and it's just me again. I try to understand everything that's happened. Now, my query to you is: am I describing surrender to the Holy Spirit in meeting for worship—or am I describing lovemaking? It might be that they are remarkably similar.

The Secret of Torture

April 2005

The spiritual consequences of secrets are sudden potholes in integrity, surprises, and struggles to keep a secret hidden rather than open and exposed to wonder—wonder being the most basic posture of spiritual life. Always, certain people will choose to be with something so challenging, to wash and heal the culture and individuals. And knowing why something exists can include many more people who listen, think, and wonder a bit to learn what torture is and what it means for a society and for people who are providers or receivers.

The spiritual consequences of torture are that you either are moved to act against it or you stifle and smolder. For each of us who have paid for torture through our taxes, the dilemma is strong. Our cultural myth of the independent individual making change and doing good encounters a fierce don't-rock-the-boat mentality in the public arena. Choosing to act in any form brings a sense of integrity and oneness with our deepest feelings of justice—always good for mental and spiritual health. It will also inevitably bring some disappointment, loneliness, and the need to explain oneself.

The choice of not acting is the more common response. Life is already full, and we tell ourselves: What might one do anyway, and aren't I in enough trouble already? It hurts to see and know what is there; we could let this one go by and forget. How much awareness do I need to maintain, anyway? The monster is too big for me to address. But both acting and not acting are work, requiring energy and effort; and only one has a payoff.

To have torture as part of the heritage the United States has provided to the world in the last several years (think of the wars in Southeast Asia and Central America, not to mention Iraq) is to experience a national loss of integrity, an ignorance, and a panic of discovery in each of our hearts—regardless of whether we approve of torture. Torture has always been easy to justify, but it resembles the addict's stash or the unwashed bruise hidden under clothing: maybe known by others, unable to be stopped, and always a greater pain than is understood.

To have U.S. leadership participate, deny, spin, and wink over the use of torture in our wars abroad lingers within us like glimpses of the car wreck that we can't get out of our minds. Torture injures all who know any aspect of it from any distance, and it shames all other good works done over hundreds of years. To do anything other than admit to it and stop it is to participate.

There is indication that torture will continue to increase. Therefore, I believe the time has come for Quakers to call a study conference on torture. The purpose would be to become informed, spread information, and choose actions of education, investigation, prevention, and treatment. Because this is a most repulsive topic, a conference may draw a small number of people at first. A conference will require careful planning, and to avoid exhausting participants it will require a measured, reflective pace. If its purpose and program are explained well, it could draw participation that included experts from a wide range of fields.

I have neither the time nor energy to create such a conference—yet I know that I cannot turn away. I ask three things of you:

Please share this call to conference widely among Friends, Friends meetings, and Friends organizations. A letter will be on my website, http://www.johncalvi.com, with future updates.

Please take this call to heart, and hold the effort in the Light.

If there are talents, gifts, or resources you or your organization have to help make this conference happen, please be in touch with me directly.

(The Quaker Initiative to End Torture- QUIT! was born May 2005 with five Friends. Our first conference with 126 attenders took place a year later. The work continues.)

A Call to Spiritual Discipline

May 2007

I was 16 years old when I came to Quaker meeting for worship the first time. Also present were a woman marathon runner, several professors, an ancient colonel from World War I, and a man who spoke Navajo and his poet wife. Not all were vegetarians or tax resisters. Not all the men had been conscientious objectors. All were white middle class people who didn't want to be part of the problems of 1968, but there was only some general agreement on how to be part of the solution.

Now, 38 years later, traveling among Friends as a teacher, I still see this odd collection of people who don't all quite fit any single description except that maybe they still want to be part of the solution to the suffering in the world.

Considering the question, what are Friends called to today? I find the answers as numerous as the various ways that Friends live their lives. On the one hand, there are the passions—the conscious and deliberate decisions and actions Friends take in their work and living. On the other hand, there are the inward spiritual practices which deepen over time. Both influence the way our lives contribute to society and help us identify the problems and the solutions.

Personally, I see a large open classroom called Life on Earth, and the shelves are full of the various learning. Some of us choose the books, some choose the math materials, and others are dancing with scarves on the round rug near the blackboard. We choose according to what catches our eye and our heart, making each choice not only valid but important. We work with our material until we understand it, and we take that knowledge to other materials. And we all move at various rates and at varying depths in ever-changing cycles. We are in motion individually, in small groups, and as The Religious Society of Friends.

We are called as watercolors are called across a page: not a simple straight line nor one shape, but many colors with densities of light, and overlapping pigment, rarely tidy. And so it is that the meat-eaters and the vegetarians work for social justice. The old and the young work against war. And men and women work against sexism, racism, and homophobia among some Friends (and maybe not so much among other Friends).

Lately, I see a fatigue among Friends in trying to sort out what is true. Can it be true that the United States needs a law to protect U.S. military personnel from protection for torture? Is what the political leaders said true, and why are their messages reported in the media without background or history to show that they are not true? There is a fatigue from witnessing the grand theft of the treasury while the basic needs of people increasingly go unmet. Yes, we see and feel the outrage among ourselves and we work locally as best we can, but our tax dollars continue to support the disasters taking place in the halls of power.

Friends today are called to put out so many fires of injustice, cruelty, militarism, and poverty; it may be that we haven't been so busy since the days of King Charles and Cromwell. If this is so, then Friends should be called to greater spiritual disciplines than ever before—spiritual disciplines because the crux of our faith is to listen for the Divine message and act upon it. Listening and acting have become more difficult as the noise of the world from suffering and the deceit has risen.

So what are the disciplines to attend to:

enough silence, listening for the Divine, trying not to hear yourself

enough rest and nurture to be clear vessels to receive Light

enough stillness to feel our humility as fragile carriers of Light

enough comfort to offer our best effort

enough strength kept up for the long haul

enough concentration to hold the focus while listening

enough love of life to see beauty while surrounded by pain

The first conference of the Quaker Initiative to End Torture in June 2006 at Guilford College in North Carolina was an open classroom like the one described above. Friends came together with interests in various aspects of the topic: history, legislation, treatment, education, and direct action. They worked individually to absorb the information, and then worked in small groups to plan actions for still larger groups. Many Friends will attend to this work, but there will be no lockstep movement with total agreement nor singular action towards one task. Rather, Friends will choose work that best fits each one's gifts and energy level. What remains unified is the intention and the spiritual discipline, aimed at staying in the Light as both seekers and carriers.

What are Friends called to do? To be good Friends and to become better Friends, especially at times when the worst potential of human nature is yet again being realized and spreading here at home.

Unobstructed Love

August 2008

Originally written for Tom Fox Was My Friend. Yours Too-
Edited by Chuck Fager May 2006

The problem with unobstructed love is that it's rarely understood. Maybe that's because it does not appear like any other love—puppy love, romantic love, true love, love of country. No, unobstructed love is unlike anything we see in day-to-day life. It is seen mostly in stories of great heroes. But even then it's so rarely witnessed that it can seem illogical, perhaps even a sickness or a chronic miscalculation.

But when the Light shines through one's soul and there becomes a certainty of what one must do, even after all the tantrums of asking that the cup pass from our lips, and the horizon one sees is suddenly more broad than ever before—well, it's not easily forgotten. The rare gift to be one with one's word, hopes, and faith washes up a dingy day and a mangy life to a spit shine inwardly and outwardly. It holds all of creation within reach of understanding and just far enough away to remain in awe.

The surrender does not come easy as it is nonverbal and lacks explanation. Whether it is a visitation, a message, or a simple knowing, the experience is a private one and known in one's heart and deep in the gut. How we shall think about it or which words to use comes about later with time and wonder and our awkward attempts to make sense of another realm.

When love has the walls around it lifted so that care and compassion are moved up and out of the rat runs of ordinary living, the transformation resembles water seeking its own level. The rules of gravity have been changed and it might be that there is no downhill and yet there is great motion and new movement and expanse.

We are spotty in our practice of unobstructed love. We try to love the ones we know we should. We might even try to love the ones we did love before something came undone. There's the duty to love the inferior and goodness knows there are slews of them. But what of loving all that is? What of loving those who might do us great harm, perhaps the ultimate harm? Could Jesus possibly have meant to Love our enemies? Surely, it's metaphor or a translation problem.

And yet, at the stage of unobstructed love, it's a simple reach. Not a simple practice, goodness knows, but once glimpsed, the temptation to feel and see that Grace again is too wondrous to await chance. No, this is an elixir beyond all.

And so it comes that a Mother Teresa, a Martin Luther King, a Daniel Berrigan, a Gandhi set off on some spiritual adventure, and the great parade of spectators haven't a clue as to the core of the adventure, not a clue—not want house and car, leave family and home, be in danger—maybe in jail or war zone? How could this not appear as madness for the merely in love?

The moments of Grace are not so rare. But the signing up for the lifetime subscription and heeding the call, that's when the crowd thins out. For the blessed few who reach that state of love and stay on, it's a ride that teaches us all how limited our vision is and how regular our hopes. This is not a ride for just anyone. There's no gift in being misunderstood by so many. No, this is a ride for a few and a message to us all that great love exists and can change hearts, move mountains and empires, and provide an edge to the known world for us to wonder at and hope the blessing comes again soon to someone.

Perfect Spiritual Work

August 2010

A perfect spiritual work should fit like a deep breath. It should bring in new life-giving energy and clear out waste. It should fill to capacity and stretch in all the right places without overwhelming. And it should be work that engages the individual as well as the corporate body.

The larger spiritual works can seem impossible at first. It won't be clear how the work can proceed as there seem to be no open doors, handles to hold, or vision to see the way clearly. It will gather only a few people to begin and slowly gather steam. And most will watch from the sidelines saying – can't be done, don't bother, fruitless folly.

What holds the work together is to see that some essence needs to be changed, cleaned, made right. This sense of essential change carries everyone on the path in some unity. Much can be disagreed with in process and practice, but the intention is held in clarity.

The Torah says- you don't have to finish this work but you shouldn't stop either. The idea that more than one generation is needed to complete the work might seem to discourage workers and yet more often than not it means the work is shared and the pressure of deadline is given the long view- do what's important now and the rest will follow.

Spiritual work is usually surrounded by reverence- a little used idea in today's culture. Reverence means that something is very very important and should be treated very carefully. By surrounding a work in reverence we know the work is special and we know how we attend to the work is done in certain perimeters of tone and practice. This often makes for less fear and conflict due to the sense of unity and common purpose.

In this way, a perfect spiritual work can mean that a daunting task takes on a delight, a welcomed challenge instead of loathsome requirement. And this dynamic generates Light for more good work. It might seem a "trick" of the Light to take a horrendously difficult work and surround it with reverence and the joy of hard work in unity. Not only unity with co-workers but unity or integrity with ones self, ones ideals. This dynamic was never understood by the forces opposing Gandhi, King, or Jesus. But has been the basis of all change done by large groups over time.

And one might wonder- is there a large spiritual work underway currently? Imagine this- The United States of America gets out of the business of war. No more undeclared wars that go on for years against tiny countries. No more spending half the budget on wars built on lies. No more of our young soldiers wounded or dead by the thousands. No more weapons manufacturers promoted by former congressmen or Pentagon generals taking overpayments to kill innocent civilians. No more US torture in our names using our tax dollars.

Holding American leadership accountable for crimes against humanity has never happened. All the American wars in Viet Nam, Latin American, and now Iraq and Afghanistan involve crimes as large as any in history resulting in large profiteering and no justice or peace.

If America is ever to be taken out of the business of war, it can begin simply on one issue- torture. There is more than enough evidence to begin investigations and prosecutions. It will take some time, some good work, and a great deal of spiritual discipline- a perfect spiritual work for a large group of seekers. Once the tide begins to be turned, all new possibilities open wide for economic justice, peaceful relations, and right use of resources.

This is a work that effects every other important issue from economy and food security to climate change and world-wide poverty in health care, clean water, and human rights. Getting the United States of America out of the business of war beginning with the investigations and prosecutions for those who ordered torture will do more to change the world in our life times than any other single issue.

And that time is now. Many torture survivors have made witness. Many documents are in the public domain. Our greatest chance for change is now. And the push for torture accountability should be made from every corner in voices too loud and numerous to ignore.

The Quaker Initiative to End Torture has a conference September 24-26 2010 at Quaker Center in Ben Lomond, CA. See – www.quit-torture-now.org We want to begin this work with your help and involvement. Please join us for a very large perfect spiritual work.

John Calvi is the founding convener of The Quaker Initiative to End Torture – QUIT. Donations can be made via www.quit-torture-now.org

Section 5

Wonder, Ponder

Luxuries and Blessings

January 2013

I am just coming back from being laid very low with three weeks of a cough and cold. I am so sick of being sick. Over the decades I've become a talented caregiver, but I am a lousy patient. Now I can breathe, which I find eminently useful, and the coughing is done, as are the druggy medicines. I was so sick I didn't visit a single thrift shop for a month!

This afternoon I was aware of being surrounded by luxury and blessings. I folded six loads of wash, while Marshall filled up the wood box with firewood and the woodstove crackled with cozy heat. We had late day massages that soothed his insomnia and calmed my cough-sore rib cage. And after dinner, I had my arm around him as we watched a "new" DVD from the Hospice thrift shop—The Green Mile.

As I stepped out into the starry night to pee, the moon was doing an incredible number with the clouds, and the moonlight on the snow shown through the piney woods surrounding our house. It's more beautiful than I have words for.

I am so happy and relieved to know and be grateful for all my blessings. And to keep in mind these simple things are great luxuries that many people go without. As the temps fall again into the single digits and the long night wind blows through the pines, I feel some care for the ones going without and a moment of reverence for all of creation. Tomorrow I pack for another trip and hope to remember all I have to share.

Crossing Borders

February 2013

When I became a Quaker at sixteen, I had no way of explaining to my Catholic parents why things felt so much more right on the far side of that border. I was only beginning to understand it myself. Looking back, one factor that truly drew me was the uncovered practice and use of reverence of Friends. It helped me to recognize what home really could be. The gathering of people for Catholic Mass and the gathering of Friends at Meeting for Worship have similar feelings of anticipation, expectation and a sense of reverence. But for me, the reverence felt more accessible and put to more active use among Friends. My frightened parents could not understand my need to change to an unknown.

I've spent much of my life crossing borders of one sort or another. Going to school meant leaving the large family enclave of an Italian working-class farm, to be with mostly middle-class WASP children and teachers in a small New England town. As a young man there was the border-crossing of my gay identity and learning about a new community I was part of. As a teacher of young children, I crossed the border of being an 'unknown stranger' who was boss of the classroom, to become a 'trusted teacher', who wanted the best for his students. This particular dynamic of gaining trust became important with respect to later work with rape survivors, people with AIDS, and with torture survivors.

All of these border crossings involved reverence. I knew that something new was waiting for me and it was very important and must be cared for with respect and gentleness. Setting aside assumption, judgment, and ignorance, to ponder with wonder, to observe, and to see meaning- I learned this was the beginning of crossing a border with reverence.

In a new country, you need to observe carefully. In my work with people who seemed at the outset very different from me, either due to imprisonment, wheelchair confinement, life expectancy, nationality, or beliefs, I had an obligation to begin with respectful observation. The obligation is part of reverence for life.

Thirty years ago, I worked with a psychotherapist on my history of incest and rape as a young child. It was difficult work as you can imagine. I was trying to bring forth feelings for release and understanding, to let these secrets stand in the Light for the first time. Just as I was up to my neck in memory and deep feeling, there came an invitation from a Canadian prison chaplain to teach massage to a group of prisoners in a maximum-security prison: a group of a dozen men convicted of murder and rape, some of them were serial rapists. My own border to cross was my fear and my lack of experience of such people. Could I not be overwhelmed by my fears, and understand the lives of these men, to know how we were part of one another? This was a steeper learning curve than I would recommend, but I was able to cross the border and come to perceive their lives, slowly and carefully. The reverence used in teaching massage—how one touches another with respect and kindness—puts all of us in a place of sensing another person's condition and caring for that other one.

Another bit of fence we must negotiate is the difference between believing and knowing. Having trust in a belief has carried many faithful through difficult times and assisted in compassionate work around the world throughout history. Knowing, by contrast, can insist on singular truths, denial of oppositional truths, and the closing of respectful observation into dismissive conclusions or condescending assumptions. Such is the nature of world history, conquest, war, and subjugation. Can we hold what we believe in deep reverence, understanding that this belief can grow and learn and change?

There are new borders to be crossed each day. Each of us must learn new things, communicate with others, do our work to get what we need and want, to be in the world. Do we have a personal culture that trespasses with disrespect or do we enter with a sincere willingness to understand and learn something with each crossing? Do we know how to move with grace even when fear or ignorance calls us to be awkward? Or are we dismissive of entire lives whose connection to us seems invisible or impossible?

I come from a very big family. I can't possibly be close to each and every one of them, but I can try to know and understand their lives when we are together. Is this easy? Of course it isn't. It's more than I can do at times. But what else are we doing that's more important? Isn't the end of disrespect the seed for healing each one of us- our homes, our nations, and our planet?

The Old Queens' Clothes

April 2013

Yes, today we took all the clothes out of the closet, every last shirt, pants, jacket, and kimono! We decided Go or Stay. I've boxed up 27 trousers, 33 shirts, and 10 coats, including 4 sports jackets, 1 leather bomber, 2 silk bombers, a raincoat, a winter parka, and 1 large wool overcoat—off to the Hospice Thrift Store.

It was like something out of the Smithsonian or the Natural History Museum. Here in the back hiding for decades are pants worn 25 years and 50 pounds ago. There is a shirt of unknown origin with a dry cleaners tag from the Reagan years. Oh, remember these pants? I loved these pants. Where the hell is this from? Your Aunt Ramona. No, no, no, you found it at a thrift shop. No, I would never bring home such an ugly kimono that wouldn't fit either of us. And see, it's real silk and very old. As my grandmother would say, *cosi brutto!* How ugly!

I can't give away the trousers I wore on my wedding day, such lush heavy cotton, a lovely cream-color. But we can keep anything we want, so good, it stays. I'll wear them one day when I'm dying and have lost half my body weight or there's a miracle of self-discipline.

Amazing how much is boxed to go. But I'm shocked by how much stays. Really, I have almost 30 white shirts? How did this happen? I have 15 pairs of trousers, all boring colors. Women get all the best colors and old short fat men, like me, we get khaki. I need more periwinkle. But nothing ever for the usual retail cost. Discounts, please. Or maybe slightly used.

I found two tuxedo shirts. One fits. I found a great old winter coat that was such a good friend through several blizzards. It was the first clothing to announce that size matters, especially at the waistline.

I have a great stash of summer clothes—wonderful short-sleeve shirts of linen and silk and cotton. And a small collection of soft light pants that float and drape on the hottest days. Oh summer, come soon! I am drowning in chill. I'm so tired of bundling up, scarf, and thick socks.

This all started when I cleaned out the sock drawer back in February. I got one bag of socks with holes and unmatched, which I put in the shed for mice to sleep in. There was another bag with ugly, nappy, worn socks for the homeless shelter. And lo, what did I find in back of the drawer—two favorite shirts that have been missing for three years. Hooray for finding them! There was a great heavy silk navy shirt with brilliant gold fish across the chest and a bright red number of thick cotton that I found in a thrift shop but have never worn. Maybe for the first time, I will only have favorite clothes. Why would I wear anything else?

Moving Old Calendar to New

February 2014

I've just been moving into my new calendar. It's a luxury and a delight to have this leather bound book that carries so much of my information and personal history each year. I have them going back 30 years and every new year I sit down for a few hours and move beloved pictures, poems, maps, along with dates and data of my upcoming trips to teach and touch around the country.

The inside cover has a picture of Joni Mitchell sitting cross-legged on top of a grand piano where Stevie Wonder sits at the keyboard. As they face the camera, she has a beautiful smirk on her face most likely from saying something very funny and he is laughing—his face bright with delight.

Then I tape three pieces of writing on a page. Walt Whitman's "When I Heard at the Close of Day"—his beautiful love poem about the great comfort of his true love coming to meet him at the coast – "For the one I love most lay sleeping by me under the same cover in the cool night." When I began my AIDS work in 1983, Whitman's notes on his nursing work in the American Civil War in DC was part of my education and training.

Then there's Shakespeare Sonnet 29—"When in disgrace with Fortune..." I love this reminder of something that is true for me during dark nights of the soul. When the voices of doubt loom large and I am fending for myself against these familiar old enemies of depression and anxiety, there is a voice in me that says, "Yeah, well, Marshall loves me!"

The third piece on this page is Jesus' Sermon on the Mount. I love this teaching and a broad interpretation that makes it a simple list of gentle reminders. I like the form enough to borrow it and make my own list of beatitudes, such as "Blessed are the tender hearted for they reveal to us our own deepest feelings."

Across from the facing page I've put a picture of Marshall with a big smile holding a beautiful cake he's made. It was his birthday and we were about to board a riverboat and take an evening cruise on the Connecticut River with some friends. Marshall is wearing a wide brimmed hat to protect from the summer sun and the lighting is just right to show the beauty of the cake and his beaming joy at this party. The photographer, John J

Meyer, has taken all the best portraits of us since we met in 1986.

Across from the Table of Contents is a photocopy of a pencil sketch by F. D. Millet. A hundred years ago as I was about to settle into Vermont as my home, a dear friend gave me this sketch that she had found at yard sale. It shows two horse-drawn hay wagons on a ferry floating across a river. It has the most wonderful sense of slow motion on a hot summer's day amidst the long heavy work of haying on a farm. She gave me this because I so obviously fell in love with it when I saw it, generous dear that she is. I kept this close to my desk as a reminder to go slow, not to push the river, to be graceful in my work, and in my being. I loved it and it affected me perhaps more deeply than any other artwork. Millet sketched it while doing some riverboat travels in Europe with some male friends soon after leaving his newly married wife back in the US.

When I met Marshall, and he invited me to join him in California to begin our life together, I had to sell almost everything to be able to afford the gas to drive across country. Selling this picture was hell and it was a blessing because it was the only thing of value I had. Now the photocopy sits in my calendar and I still gaze at it with much love.

Several pages in I've a copy of Billie Holiday's lyrics to "Comes Love." It gives testimony that there is nothing to do when loves comes but to give up and surrender. "Don't try hiding, cause it isn't any use, cause you'll start sliding, when your heart turns on the juice... Comes love, nothing can be done."

Two pages of weights and measurement conversion charts are covered with Seamus Heaney's poem, "From the Republic of Conscience", that was sent to me by Pete Seeger. It's a declaration of participation in simplicity and democracy to all humanity.

Then comes the almost two hundred pages of calendar with every chance that I will remember where and when I've promised to be for a year.

At page 170 I've covered up a restaurant chart with a large print of poems by Wu-mei (1250 BC) and Rumi (1270 AD), both reminding me to slow down and notice those things not of this world. On the page across, are two pictures from a favorite beach hotel in California. There has always been something about strolling on a beach that clears out my own personal chaos.

At page 194 there's a chart to mark birthdays and anniversaries. I've 50 dates marked to celebrate family and friends. Beside these are poems by Rumi, Johanna Jordan, and Hung Tzu. Rumi mentions Jesus' drive to do healing. Johanna draws us to listen to the "great hum" of the universe within us. Hung Tzu says, "A true heart can cause snow to fly on a summer's day, but a hypocrite when alone, his body and shadow are ashamed of each other."

On 209 is a picture of our wedding day by Riley Robinson. It's a great portrait with us beaming in fancy clothes on a bright summer's day. There's also a map of North America. I love maps. I have two atlases at my desk and two at my bedside nightstand.

On the last pages of this calendar book are pictures of the globe in three positions so as to see each continent in bright colors, a great Annie Leibovitz portrait of Pete Seeger with his banjo standing along the edge of his beloved Hudson River. He's looking at the horizon upriver and smiling. And there's a postcard map of the Caribbean.

Once, when my annual rest was being interrupted by a number of crises of good friends and I was heading for certain collapse, Marshall announced that I must pack for the beach in the dead of winter because he'd cashed in all our frequent flyer miles and was taking me away for my own health and safety.

I'd never been to an island and certainly not to the Caribbean. It was a two-fold paradise: no one to care for and a tiny island with six beaches to stroll. It saved my life and this postcard reminds me that there are more islands to explore.

There is the floor plan to the famous Gamble House by Greene and Greene in Pasadena, California. This house is the opposite of mine. Theirs is large and spacious. Every aspect of it has been thought out, planned for, and had numerous craftsmen attend to its function and great beauty. Our house is cozy and friendly. And there is not single corner or aspect that is finished or couldn't be improved upon by care, craftsmanship, and cash.

The last page is a map of the US. It is without political boundaries, no state lines. It features the geographical realms of mountains and plains and rivers and coastlines and altitudes. It makes me want to drive cross country to all the places I have not yet been and to see the vistas from high up and travel the valleys of unknown rivers.

Here I sit in my loft office surrounded by four desks facing the big south windows with the sun streaming in on a bright, deep winter day. It's over 90 degrees in this little passive solar house, while outside the temps struggle to get above 20 over a new foot of snow. I'm wearing a smidgen of cotton and sweating like a farm animal, as I've taken all these things from the old calendar and put them in the new. All of this makes me very happy and feeling ready for a new year. I have favorite things to travel with and reminders of beauty and patience and kindness. All these will go with me to places of great hurt, where fear and anger have sway over the human heart. And I will attempt to bring word that even as it is very hard, the world is still beautiful.

Of Two Minds

January 2014

Sitting here on a cold winter's night in our snug little house so warm and cozy a few days before husband returns, I am noticing something that makes me wonder. There are days when I mainly remember my mistakes, the times I did something embarrassing or wrong, the accidents of awkwardness or ignorance or simply wasn't careful, or chose to be stupid or mean.

And then there are the days I remember my accomplishments, my competence, my successes such as they are, and when I've been of help and done the right things, made the right choices.

These are two completely different experiences, at least at first. They are different, in part, because of my reaction to them, and whether I involve mercy. So much of my life I've remembered the things I've done wrong and felt bad all over again, as though it's just happened a second time. It's such a familiar feeling, such a given, so known.

Whereas to remember what I've done right feels newer, less sure, and maybe even a bit suspect, because it almost doesn't feel original. Yet, to know that I've done right- feels more whole, more of who I actually am, and more true.

I know where the bad feeling comes from. I was thoroughly trained, completely ordained to the bad feelings by adults unhappy with themselves. The good feeling, that sense of self that includes not only some sense of competence but also of mercy in self viewing, was where I began life. I then had to find my way back to it.

I know these paths as surely as I know the contours of my own body or how far the water glass is on my nightstand. They have been the trails up and back, over and down my entire life. Sorting them out to understand and have some control has taken forever and still it seems I am on the ride one way or the other before I've made a choice. Then I have to become aware, learn where I am, wonder how I got here, and choose the more positive way.

Just this amount of knowing has taken a lifetime. I'm just getting it sorted out and really I'm not that far from having to pack up and leave. It doesn't feel fair to spend so much time trying to get free and get well and know goodness and happiness deeply before they settle in as familiars. Now the task is remembering what I know, not losing track, and finding the door, again and again.

Does mastery of my own inner mechanics bring delight, relief, some sense of further accomplishment? Yes, at times. Does a migraine ever really feel like a good teacher or just a painful enforcer of necessary learning? Learning what to do with trouble, conflict, pain is important life learning and the learning is always good.

I am grateful for the moments, the islands of contentment. I have at times forgiven those whose trespasses crippled so much of my young person. There is some peace to it all. But a bad dream or a flash of memory suddenly forces back a discipline of knowing what to do when that negative dark surrounds and tries to convince that all is lost.

All has never been lost. It's been hell for a time. There've been times that seemed to have no possible way out. But being strongly stubborn, I've always just hung on until the storm passed. And it's always passed. It's never gone forever, just made breaks, sometimes long breaks. And the breaks are longer now.

Tonight on a very peaceful quiet night, I'm noticing these things, things I've known forever, things inside me like blood and bone that have always been and will always be. Now maybe I can see them a bit more clearly and my life has less trouble.

Two Wants, Neither Friends

March 2014

I have two images playing in my head lately- two images of myself and what I desire. They are opposing images. The first is that I live in a grand house and can offer refuge to many people. I make wonderful meals and offer comfort to the weary and wounded. There is peace and safety and generous hospitality. There's a feeling that my love is bountiful and there cannot be too much, because the need is great among people. I love the feeling of trust and providing to the life wounded. I feel this deeply and find small ways of expressing it in my much smaller life and in a small house, nowhere near the image and day dream that comes to me at times.

The other image is that I have one large clean and clear desk near the window on a beautiful quiet day. I take some fine writing paper and create a letter to a friend describing my feelings of peace and contentment in the luxury of the moment- alone, feeling my feelings clearly, and without schedule or demand. This image brings me a great longing for simplicity and no demands on my time or feelings, just the restfulness of time to write something true for myself to send to one person. This is also far beyond my reality and not within reach on most days in my life.

The idea of providing hospitality to a few or many has always intimidated me. But I see such need for safe harbor and comfort. I've learned to cook a bit and I love to make a delicious meal for people who are hungry. I appreciate the art of creating good food. I've never lived in a big house where I could take in strays and make many welcomed. This is a newish image to me. I've always wanted to help the wounded all my life and it seems to me that the need for sanctuary increases each year. But the idea of making a big home to do so is oddly new. I imagine myself doing it as an old person, old and cuddly, a gay fairy godmother making safety, cookies, encouragement or stern lecture, as needed.

The longing for a clear desk and lovely writing paper with many days and no demands is somehow an older and truer dream. This idea suits my daily energy better and in some ways is more of who I am now. I tire from the complication of lots of people around me. I crave the quiet, the stillness, and the sounds of the forest around me without interruption.

And so this very late night I am wondering about these two ideas within me. I do each in my own small ways, but they are not friends within me. I do want to offer a safe house and home, but I can't. I do want the simple life of quiet and stillness without the noise of the world and endless people. I want the order of good writing paper on a clear desk and a beautiful late morning to send loving greetings to a dear one sincerely from my heart. And this is all too rarely possible in my life as it is now constructed. I am happy some days just to find the beautiful wood of my desks through all the stacks of undone work and the impatient projects and the demands of a busy life.

I suppose I am craving ideals and ideal settings in both instances. I want to do each in superior ways with excellent outcomes. In truth I am at a loss to achieve either very well. The hug and kiss I can offer is good but fleeting. The quiet moment to write is often, as it is now, well past midnight when I've grown tired of other work. Should I have designed a different life? Am I not combining what I have in the right ways or percentages? Is this simply a way of seeing I am tired? I want both. I can't organize either. Reaching for either seems impossible. I must polish the stones I have, none of which I complain about here. I have a life of amazing choices. Maybe I am just old and tired and not making enough time to do nothing. Is that it? Is that what I see after all this mucking about in the dark corners of my wee brain? Or perhaps a new stage of life in my early 60's is dawning and shifts are to come.

Lonely, Adored, and Good

Summer 2013

I've been thinking how three feelings are connected. I've been working with some people on their loneliness and the difficulty of not feeling their goodness and how instead of being adored, they were betrayed. It seems to me that everyone needs to be adored. This is not just a simple matter of the ego wanting. Being adored is a basic human need that hopefully many of us experience early on. But attached to this need is the experience of feeling lonely when being adored is interrupted. I think loneliness is the biggest problem in the world. Lots of people will tell you it's greed, but I think if you look in back of greed you will find loneliness, that fear of not having enough.

When we are betrayed, especially early on in life, the experience of being adored is interrupted. Out of this comes not only the feeling of loneliness, but maybe also loosing touch with a sense of our own goodness. The sting of betrayal can cause doubt about being worthy, about our goodness. That need to be adored is complicated by the pain of betrayal and having less sense of our goodness. Our ability to receive love may be obstructed by wounds, fear, and worry. That sense of goodness might feel starved or worse, disconnected from us.

It gets quite messy quickly. We need the regular giving and receiving of love as one of the main ways to gather a sense of our goodness. Being adored is the basic part of this. As this is damaged or slowed, loneliness and a loss of that sense of goodness is all too common. As it is a painful experience, receiving love begins to feel risky, maybe too risky.

It's a tight little circle that is either spiraling up or spiraling down. That's why simple kindness has such power. We might halt a fast descent spiraling downward with some simple compassion. Just a change of tone, some certainty of goodness or care being felt may have a profound effect. Even a small gift of kindness can save a day, save someone's hope, a life.

The Trouble with Summer

August 2013

I think the trouble with summer is that we grow up learning summer means summer vacation. When I was growing up, this meant summer on my grandmother's farm with dozens of cousins coming to stay for weeks at a time. There were long, hot days with tons of things to do - picking and eating fresh cherries from the hillside above Uncle Nick's house, bringing in hay from the fields, swimming in the pond, helping to bring an escaped cow back to pasture, watching an animal birth, coming into the cool stone house my grandfather built to eat the fabulous homemade bread, butter, and jams my grandmother had made.

As one who hated school, summer also meant that invaluable gift of unscheduled time, the lushness of playing hide-and-seek well into dark, the big empty day with time for anything and everything. No rushing.

I don't know if it's biological or environmental, but my body clock still says summer is that lush time of open space and freedom from schedule. But my reality conflicts with this terribly. Now I wake up to the fabulous heat and sunshine of another great summer day in Vermont. Generally, I am already late, behind on tasks to be done, overwhelmed by the timing of the world expecting things. But internally, I see and feel summer deep in my soul and want to wander off doing nothing for weeks at a time.

That's not the worst part. Now it is mid-August and the signs of summer leaving have already begun here in Vermont. This reminds me of so many old boyfriends ages ago. They would pursue me and then discover what a wreck of a human I was and flee. I was left standing there saying, "But I love you so much, why are you going?" And that's exactly how I feel about summer each and every August as the days shorten and the nights cool and you know what's coming.

I love summer so much that I could be very happy to have summer year round. I know this is heresy in this part of the world. Maybe it's just the start of a cranky old age. Or it's the deeply worn brain patterns of the beginning of school and the start of depression anticipating the dark days of early winter and bad grades. Or is it really my Italian blood screaming for me to be in a Mediterranean climate?

No matter. The end of summer breaks my heart. I feel jilted and heart broken that my love leaves me to cold winds, dead leaves, and temperatures of meanness without mercy. How many years will this nonsense go on in my small mind? How many late springs will find me flinging myself into love again, lost to all sensual delight, and in another deep end of attachment and devotion to the temporary? What other fleeting realities do I allow to add to my confusion and pain?

Watching Myself and You

June 2013

A thunderstorm is lighting up the sky this evening on a trip far from home. The clouds have held great drama. Rain and hail and warm wind going cooler have washed the late day into night. I've done two loads of wash, one by machine and another by hand. And now have ironed 7 shirts and 2 pair of pants. I am recalling the past few days and all the parts and pieces that have made this short stop on a long trip so good, kind, and restful. I lived here 33 years ago. Every part of the city holds some memory of life in my early 30's. Dear friends, co-conspirators, and seekers of all manner were my teachers as I came here to discover my gift as a healer/teacher. The love of many people here created my life.

A visit with a friend shows me his age and his gift for community and compassion. His bakery saved my meager life back when his offer of work meant a supper, hours of the rock music 100 countdown, and some cash for washing muffin tins at midnight. His tamales are the best for miles and some will come with me tomorrow as I leave.

Another dear one has been teaching Tai Chi around the nation. His grace and manner are matched by his keen observations and his gift to laugh at himself as he seeks the higher ground. He used to run up and into the mountains. Now he teaches old Russian Jewish women Big Cloudy Hands. They all know this is very special.

Then I have time with a maverick, whose years on earth were once an occasion for all things debauched. If it was good enough for Siddhartha, it was good enough for him. Now he raises daughters. He sees and knows how precious life is and how carefully one must steer oneself and, when possible, one's children. His gift of teaching himself and now young ones has grown into mastery well beyond his exploits of sensation and bad boy delights.

I have a late breakfast with one who has lived the wild life and seems not to have aged in her face one teensy bit. She's come round to longing for a bit less wildness and more of tender intimacy. She has grown into professional competence despite of numerous obstacles. Her joy in living remains clear and loud and irresistible.

Now comes a call from Marshall and some news. He's become executive director of a company he joined less than two years ago. Hooray that all his good work, talents, skills, and gifts are well used and recognized. He makes me so proud. I am so happy for him to have all this honor and accomplishment.

He shares news that his father, who will soon be 90, visited a World War II museum far from home. There on the wall is a big picture of him standing guard over Hermann Göring during the Nuremburg trials. His father's stories have been slow to come out.

I pack up tomorrow after a few days rest and continue my work trip for another week. There is a workshop of 50 people for deep relaxation and healing from trauma, a reading from my new book, and some teaching about American torture. In my mind, I play the movie of my life to recall how many parts and feelings move through each day. To love my life feels slowly more natural as I crawl into old age, trying to remember that great thing I realized just a moment ago.

Is That the Toilet Ringing?

September 2013

Well I just want to say that if I did happen to drop my cell phone down my compost toilet this morning it was very wise of me to hire the young farmer next door to rebuild the big hatch door that I use to empty the thing out every 6 or 8 years because he put a big hinge on the oversized lid and it pops open easier than a Budweiser and this is very good because when I tried to go in through the toilet seat the ratio of shoulder proportions to toilet opening registers clearly even after you've used the landline to call yourself and you can hear the little bugger ringing somewhere nearby and just a tad muffled by goodness knows what and you reach in thinking it's just got to be near the top and of course just below the sawdust is something else I just put there recently to my great relief but now of course it's in the way and I start to get nauseous and really why wouldn't I but I'm sure if I can just reach a bit more but then I hang up on myself because I'm not answering and so I call again but first hands must be scrubbed and so back into the house and back out again which is when I rip off the top of the toilet and the big 18 inch square opening looms like a cave nobody wants to go in and it's still too far to quite reach so of course I have to go outside and see about opening the hatch that sits just downhill from the house like a basement door but different cause there's no dry storage here no siree but the good news is that the hatch isn't glued down and lifts open easily and all I have to do is climb on to this small mountain of what country people like myself demurely call "night soil" which is quite different from what you are imagining which is some tank sloshing with stink and awfulness but it's really a big heap of dry sawdust with a tuffs of toilet paper sticking out like lights on a Christmas tree but less bright and I reach in with the rake to take off the top of the mountain but a shiny bit caught my eye off to the side sitting neatly on a lump of sawdust was my beloved iPhone that had fallen out of my bathrobe pocket as I scooped some sawdust to cover my morning donation not realizing that I'd made a surprising technological deposit at the same time which then tobogganed down the slope to a nice dry resting place awaiting me patiently like a Zen lesson to say no it's not the worst but the day is young!

Section 6

On the Road

John's Universal Laws of Travel

So you are going across country. Good weather's come. You've put some cash together and you are leaving for a while to go who knows where or how. You are young and this is your first time. Hooray that you are joining a great tradition. Yes, a tradition. You are inventing nothing but your own life. Going off willy-nilly pedal to the floor without a steering wheel or a map is nothing new. But it is marvelous and so I am giving you some ideas to take to heart about this adventure that is new as you and older than me. I give you these out of love, knowing your trip will be different from every other ever taken. They come from miles and years of travel.

I personally exhausted no less than 3 Volkswagen buses going cross-country. I took Greyhound from New York City to Portland, Oregon, and had an Amtrak tour of the Midwest that would've killed a lesser person. I have crossed more than one border illegally, been arrested for illegal sleeping, and hitchhiked illegally away from that courtroom. So listen to these, my universal rules of travel. See which are true and which are the ramblings of just another old gay Italian Quaker.

Always make plans in pencil and make sure you have a big eraser.

Never miss today's beauty wondering about tomorrow's destination.

Always carry a journal to write your fascinating history in, gum to improve your own or your friend's breath, and plenty of water so you can flush away the old you.

Suspect every one of something wonderful or dreadful and expect new friends daily.

Don't be nice to anyone who pisses you off, except the police.

Yes, there are differences between people but most often they are not the differences we first think are there and they are usually the differences we all hold in common.

No matter how logical it seems, never say, "How much is this in real money?"

The best hitchhiking sign I ever used said simply, "Harmless".

The healthiest thing about travel is how it reduces your life to taking care of right now, today, the great immediacy of living this moment. Let your feelings roll with the changes and don't hold on to a feeling as it leaves.

Old luggage doesn't get stolen, so never buy new.

Wear your favorite clothes all the time. Why, pray tell, do we own anything else in the way of clothing?

Feeling foreign can be done at home or even by yourself. Don't allow this mistaken perception to separate you from yourself or others.

Avoid looking like you just bought everything new for this trip.

Listen and watch for signs from angelic intervention to guide you at forks in the road. It's only a roll of the dice if you're not listening.

You may have to carry everything, so don't take much or buy much.

If God, or one her helpers, tells you to buy an old suitcase, don't argue. Don't think old means tasteless. There's nothing worse than ugly baggage be it family history or 1963 orange American Tourister.

If you are truly wandering, take one big piece of luggage, a smaller one for day trips, and something handy to keep your essentials in.

Find out what people lived in a place first and some other history.

Remember, thrift stores are not only for the poor, but for the hopeful.

Nomadic tribes have wonderful and awful sayings about the rest of us who live in one place. An old gypsy saying is, "*Gaeje* live all their lives lying on one side." Of their own lives they say, “We are a candle that is all flame and no wax."

Spend time looking over maps like you do a newspaper. Notice the headlines and what catches your attention.

If you want to get rid of someone, use the old Lowara gypsy trick of coughing a lot and scratching yourself all over.

Always leave your rooms clean and say "thank you" to the building.

Sex, drugs, and rock n' oll is not a quaint saying any more than the Iron Curtain, multinational corporations, or air pollution are travel slogans. All of these are extreme realities. The point is to have some idea of the edge and not go over it.

Boredom is your own fault. It's the worst thing a traveler does to himself or the people around them.

Always send postcards and tell the truth about the trip without whining or lying.

Remember that you can't always improve a situation, but you can certainly make it worse.

Always surround yourself with people and things that are strong and beautiful in a variety ways.

Remember it's easier to be nice than nasty, but don't forget nasty.

Balance the giving and receiving you do in someone's home.

Remember people don't mean much of what they say, until they have some regard for you.

Be sure you spend some time near water and light everyday.

Listen for the music in a place, be it voices, wind, or a recording.

Say "thank you" to vehicles, boats, and anyone else who gets you where you are going.

If you see someone's pain, remember it is not yours. But parts of it may seem familiar.

If you help someone or someone helps you, don't be surprised.

Losing every thing happens every day to someone, when your turn comes, scream only for a few days.

Don't get stuck in any one thing without a rest from it. Things like happiness , snow, food, moving, sound,

Remember, whatever you are being greedy with will disappear.

Eating when you are hungry and lying down when you are tired are the two biggest luxuries in the world.

Love the road and the going as well as the place you stay.

Living on the road is no excuse for smelling like you do, so wash.

Change is always the biggest part. Give it a kiss and say, "thank you."

Going West

September 13 – October 16, 2010

Friday 9/10. Preparations Towards the West

In a few days, I will leave Putney, Vermont to drive across country and host the 4th Quaker Initiative to End Torture—QUIT! at Quaker Center in Ben Lomond, California September 24-26. I would very much appreciate it if you could, during this time, hold this effort in the Light and keep this important work in your prayers. It is our hope to begin turning a tide and in time, with much good work, save some lives. Thank you for your every peaceful moment of keeping us in mindful reverence. In gratitude, John—Founding convener, QUIT

Sunday 9/12. Packing It All

I've been wearing too small underwear for a week and socks that don't match and shirts with wingspan lapels. Why? Well, because I'm going away for a month and have to save all my good clothes for traveling. I got the car checked out. Seventeen-inch tires cost a lot more then sixteen-inch tires. Would never have guessed that extra inch cost so much. Two trips to the Laundromat. Now I've chosen favorite luggage, bedding, and cleared my desks of all the traveling parts, and the car trunk hasn't room for an ant to pee. None.

A computer bag, an office bag, a box of handouts, a bedding duffle, 4 suitcases- each with 5 days' worth of clothes, a shoe bag full of sneakers, a nice clean wastebasket full of toiletries, a box of snacks, a lovely leather bag with journal & water colors & stationary & favorite pens &—it just goes on and on.

This morning while packing clothes I was doing OK, right through T-shirts, socks, underwear, robes, bathing suits, belts, and shoes. Tidy, well chosen, and my best, such as it is. But when I got to pants and shirts, cracks in my systems broke down. I had laid the various suitcases out in the bedroom and was stacking clothes in piles of 5 days each. The shirts began to confuse me right away. Looking at the suitcases I say to myself,

"You only need a few in each suitcase, a few long sleeve for evenings and a few short sleeve as it's still warm everywhere you are going." But I'll probably see snow in Bozeman.

But then I'm suddenly sure I need to bring my favorite shirts to look my best. So I begin to sort them out by type. Why do I have 25 white shirts? Well, because I don't much like to choose what I'm going to wear every day at home. Years ago I adopted a uniform of jeans and a white shirt. I get up, I put them on. I don't have to think about it- simple and tasteful. Think 4-H/GAY, a Neanderthal fashion rut. Every time I see a white shirt on sale, it's mine.

Then of course I want to wear my blue shirts because they bring out my eyes. When you have no eyebrows because you took after your eyebrow-less mother, anything that sets off the eyes is very good. Besides, I love blue. So, OK. The best blue shirts have to come, too—the two dress button-downs, that fabulous navy silk one.

Since I'm going to be in some very warm places I'll need to bring the linen shirts too- that fabulous blue one, the 5 white short sleeve ones, and the 2 or 3 long sleeve ones. Thank you thrift shops of America!

That's how it went until the suitcases looked like stuffed pigs leaking sleeves and cuffs. I did put a few things back. But then I decided that instead of wearing schlock to drive in, saving the good stuff for when I'm teaching, I just had to look like a gentleman while driving. Suddenly white shirts were put into position along with those wonderful silk/linen pants and the stylish Puma sneaks. Yes, I would look the part of a gentleman, a big old queen gentleman with a big black leather purse overstuffed with sunglasses and hankies and cell phone and maps. Marshall watches this like an anthropologist observing a new tribe; what might they be called? Marilynwannabes? Bigolqueensilk&linens? Can'tdecidetakeitalls? I've seen Marshall pack for 2 weeks work in Europe in 20 minutes, using one bag, and looking fabulous the whole time. I will schlep enough suitcases for an airliner, wear 1/5 the stuff, and look nearly passable.

How has this happened that I'm going away for just over a month to work in 5 states and to drive at least 8,000 miles? Usually I get an invitation to teach and travel for a weekend or a week and then come home. And I often make twenty or more trips a year this way. This trip was different. First, there's the QUIT conference in Ben Lomond. When I'm out west I like to work at Dragonfly Transitions in Klamath Falls. Marshall was going to have a week's vacation at the end of the QUIT conference. Could he join me and we go south to see his folks? But that would mean renting a car and buying airline tickets and it would cost too much. Could I get work on the way going west and coming back east? Yes, 4 Quaker meetings—Missoula, Tucson, Santa Fe, and Albuquerque were very welcoming. Way opened.

Thursday 9/9. The Best Cases

I suppose it began with my childhood daydreams of running away. I dreamed about what I'd take with me, some sparse collection of things I could carry and what would I put them in. That's when containers first interested me- the sack, the suitcase, the large basket, the leather bag. When I left home at 18, I had an old wicker basket my grandmother had repaired with a piece of clothesline. That was it. Soon, as I traipsed about from rent to rent, working in the bowels of Yale University's Science Hill, I had a backpack and a very large basket that carried all my clothes, even when I lived in that first VW bus.

Then old suitcases began to show up, mostly Samsonite. One would appear and speak to me of a trip I was about to take, though I didn't know it. I acquired about 20 of them and had a traveling work before I gave most of them up to an AIDS auction.

It was maybe a decade later that the addiction began to show—leather bags. It began at a yard sale in Boulder. A woman was selling a small leather backpack made of beautiful supple brown leather. I loved the feel of it and how it collapsed when empty and was so beautiful when full. Since then I have collected a dozen leather bags and my favorite kind of trip is where I can pack and load the car with all of them.

This makes no sense, least of all to me. I can't even imagine what could have happened in a former life to make packing into beautiful leather bags such an extreme delight. It's somehow akin to playing with Barbie dolls or trucks in the sandbox. Some object is infused with a projection by its possessor. This makes it important beyond measure and thereby giving me great joy. I do something similar with Joni Mitchell music, antique cars, and fine writing paper.

Now I am about to drive away for a month, enjoy several climates, and will need to dress for both work and play and heat and cold. *Et, voilà.* Numerous leather bags are necessary. Today I packed 3 leather shave kits to go into 3 leather garment bags, all second hand found in numerous thrift shops across the land. I'll use the small brown garment bag, good for a few shirts and pants, and the large black garment bag, good for a week of clothes with room for shoes and towels. Plus one more so I can pack 3 bags for 5 days of clothes. I'll use the oversized doctor's bag, tan with long loop handles. Then a shoe bag—the big red tote with snaps that will hold more shoes than I own and a bag for jackets- sport coat, silk bomber, denim jacket, and another to hold linens, pillows, and blankets. There's that great oversized black brief case for the laptop and other electricals.

Other itinerant teachers/preachers worry about what they'll say. What I've been given to teach is more certain in me than my bones. So I am left wondering if I chose the best cases for this trip.

Monday 9/13. A Visit to Begin the Journey

It was difficult to leave Marshall this morning in Putney. A sad, long hug and kiss goodbye only made me want to stay home more. But we both have full days and weeks ahead, cooking hot on the front burner, so off we went, he to his college and me to the interstate. I drove over 400 miles today and the last person I saw going the speed limit was Marshall.

Late in the afternoon the internet map failed to direct me to a retirement home where an old friend now resides. I wandered around several towns in the area, having to backtrack some, stopping and asking directions twice, and finally arriving hours late. She is a grand dame in the best sense—scholar, teacher, philanthropist, and pushy old Quaker lady. She had been a great mentor to me. Her recollections of her debut into society are of a time long past.

I was uneasy in making this visit, as I had not seen her since her mind began to leave. It was going to be difficult to see a razor sharp mind and energetic peace worker let out to pasture earlier than others due to mental and physical health. What would my old friend be like when not herself anymore? Would she remember me and us being friends for nearly 40 years?

Partly it was a delight and joy to be with her again—the smart, naughty rebel from high society of decades past still loved a good story, still remembered much of the past, still eager to know what is shaking the world from the bottom up. Her own court case, conscientious tax exemption, almost made it to the US Supreme Court but for the lawyer who choose the wrong defense, as she had told him beforehand.

But the visit was also sad. She was hobbled, no short-term memory, easily tired, and lacking intellectual vigor. She lived in single room with a half dozen antiques. Her many-roomed house is gone now. Her charge into justice and peace work is halted. Her finances, at one time lush, are now taken up with doctors and medicines and aides in an old people's home. While she puts on a brave face and says how grateful she is for this and that, it's clear that she is feeling somewhat demeaned by how life is turning out. She is well enough to feel how the diminishment has been sudden and without choice, though done as gracefully as possible. I tell her the best stories I can think of to make her laugh. She remembers more than I expected, although she also covers well, pretending to remember sometimes.

The visit is a mix. I love seeing her again and noticing what is still vital. It's also sad, because she did not want a dotage. She wanted to work and struggle and help until it was over. Now she spends a lot of time sitting by the window.

Back in the car for another couple of hours going west. I sup in a bar with a sports network blaring and the guys at the bar doing regular guy talk. It reminded me of the years growing up with my father and older brothers and how utterly boring straight white boys can be when there is only talk of cars and football- yawn, yawn. I learned from two uncles that there was such a thing as a life of the mind, where one wondered, sought to know more, and understood how things are connected. My mentors have been seekers with great intellect, who worked to untie the knots of pain and confusion in the world in various ways—strong minds, large compassion, disciplined, graceful. They have been a great gift.

Tuesday 9/14. Best Parts

A favorite part of driving cross-country is the large open space where my mind can wander. I am away from all routine and schedule. I love to have some time with no music, all the windows open, and just allow thoughts to blow through.

I began preparing a plenary speech this morning as I drove through the Alleghany Mountains. The wide open valleys and long ridges were beautiful. Soon the landscape opened up to the wide beautiful farmland of Ohio. I saw several Amish carriages this day- it made me drive slower and wonder about life at such a pace as a horse and wagon. I wondered about old friends, whereabouts unknown. I thought about some news on neurology might be part of my understanding of torture, particularly sexual abuse. I saw many barns over the last 800 miles and find I like the old stone barns best. But if I ever build a dream house, it will be a stone and wooden barn, grand and simple.

Hosted in Ohio this night by a friend who gives excellent hospitality. This is a gift that is so special while on the road. She's made a small cottage into a whirl of color and beautiful spaces and full gardens and a kitchen bursting with wonderful foods for catering and friends. The rescue animals feel safe and loved here, as do I. She's made a life and a home with all the parts and pieces that causes admiration and delight. There is a good balance of community, giving/receiving, and well connected/well used. No one would ever guess this college chaplain used to be a Harvard professor of the history of science.

Tomorrow I'll have 9 hours on the road, see more beautiful farmland, and avoid Chicago. Then on to Madison for a visit with two men I've never met but have been in touch with for almost 30 years. My car goes too fast sometimes- 90 feels like 60. This is not good. I must learn restrain, at least until I get to bigger states.

Wednesday 9/15. An Adventure in Madison

A hundred years ago, in 1981, I left being a Montessori teacher of young children after 8 years and went to massage school. I put a notice in the gay Quaker newsletter saying I'd appreciate any help. And lo, out of the Midwest came four bottles of massage oil from a gay couple. They had begun a business of soaps and lotions and oils and were very kind to me. There was some correspondence over the 30 years, but we'd never met or spoken. Now I'd written asking to sleep on their couch as I rocketed through Madison to Missoula.

More perfect hosts have never been known. They met in 1969 and have been partners in romance and business since. They are kind and sweet and fun. They feel like old friends very soon. They make me welcome and give me a house tour after some visiting on the kitchen terrace overlooking treetops and the city. From the outside, the house looks like a very modern brownstone, a city house mostly vertical. Inside, the core is a stairway that continually brings you to new spaces on new levels. I lose count of the rooms, but it's one of those houses that is so beautiful that you hear a voice in your head saying, "I don't care what they say, I'm not leaving." The care and attention to detail is beyond what I've ever known. I'll just say that the built-in desk in the guest room is made of onyx—Yes, child, pure black quartz polished like a mirror. For one accustomed to peeing outdoors, the guest bathroom with marble sink and granite shower make a lasting impression. Does one visit again with adoption papers in hand?

Friday 9/17 Beauty and the Beast

The Great Plains across southern Minnesota and South Dakota are beautiful. I can imagine Black Elk and a large group of Sioux moving along the horizon or great herds of buffalo. The land is so large and goes on forever off into the horizon. It is at once intriguing and overwhelming. Like the ocean without land, I want to see it and know it, but with some sort of tether connecting me to something familiar. It would help to be 20 feet tall or to be able to fly. There is so much to take in. It calls me to go off the main roads and into new places. The scale makes me feel small. It's a good humbling. In some ways I feel like some gawking Yankee from the tiny, cozy Northeast lost in the spaciousness. The hours of driving piled up into long days and evenings. The spaces are so much bigger here, the possible stops fewer and farther between. I do 90 mph in South Dakota in the slow lane.

The check engine light came on about 10 p.m. in the tiniest of towns, with another 100 miles to Rapid City. Maybe the light is nothing. The closest Saab dealer, in Billings, is five hours away. I need to get to Missoula by Saturday noon. I'm on I-90 west for Billings, then friends in Bozeman, then Missoula. Car runs fine. How strong is Quaker Light around engine stuff? I pretend not to be anxious.

Sunday 9/19. Mountains, Snow, and Warm Welcome

What are the odds that one can be 2,000 miles in to an 8,000 mile trip, have a serious car repair needed, still able to drive the car before the repair, find that the only Saab dealer in three states is on the way to my next stop, find they would have the part I need, have time in their schedule to make the repair, AND lose no time in my schedule of 21 stops to teach in five states in 33 days? What are the odds? I think a gazillion to one! But that's what happened. Car's fixed, I'm on schedule, credit card is in shock, and I'm back on the road.

When one is going up a mountain pass and the temperatures suddenly drop and one wonders if the mist is going to be snow and ice at the top—this is a great time to reach into one's big old queen purse and pull out a Liz Chocolate Chip cookie!

It was a quick overnight in Bozeman, where it began to snow as I entered the home of Marshall's dear childhood friend. She and her husband have made a detailed and scholarly study of the geology, botany, and zoology of Yellowstone National Park. They know tons of things about the history going back thousands of years and various stories about people as the land moved from exotic wilderness to a much visited site of awe. They are a delight to be with. I am made very welcome and my bedroom views a range of mountains that are just gathering snow. Yes, they say, I might run into more snow on the top of the "hill" on my way to Missoula—top of the hill indeed! In Vermont this would be our highest summit. I try not to take the snow as an insult of personal rudeness. It is only the 3rd week of September, for goodness' sakes.

In Missoula, I am hosted in the most wonderful fashion with a lovely dinner and a great group from Missoula Meeting for two workshops and a QUIT Update this afternoon and evening. My host is a new friend who feels like an old friend. Her home is very homey and I'd like to stay longer. It's good to be in Missoula, again. The welcome here is very warm. Guests coming from far away are treated as very special. When I attended North Pacific Yearly Meeting here last year, the setting of the town between peaks with several rivers washing down slopes and valleys seemed a perfect place to settle in from the open Great Plains. I can envision living here easily. All the good people here make it easy to do.

The Missoula Friends Meetinghouse is a small, former church in a sweet neighborhood of little ranch houses. The meeting room is almost square with three or four rows of benches facing inward from each wall. A sense of good people meeting reverently is clear in this room with a high ceiling. Friends in the large western states, especially those states of low population, have a more reverent sense of the value of every Friend, unlike very crowded brotherly cities where you can't throw a brick without hitting some Mainliner.

Yearly meetings in the large, sparse states can feel more like a small town than other yearly meetings and this makes for a more intimate personal setting in seeking the way forward. In some ways it's similar in their very early days with Friends for Lesbian and Gay Concerns in that we don't get to have meeting with "our own kind" in a large group until Summer Gathering or Midwinter. Gypsy encampments in Europe before WWII were broken up by locals, the wagons were led to crossroads and directed to go in multiple directions so as to break up the concentration. They always knew they'd meet later on down the road. But they also knew how precious time together was. There is something in the nature of small, scattered groups that reminds us how sparse and fragile life is and how good it is to be together when we can.

I took some pics with my iPhone, but don't know where they disappear to. I haven't had time to see how my new phone works. I wish I were taking more pics of the wonderful people I meet along my way.

Monday 9/20. Secrets and Silence

There's been a study in high contrast for me this trip. Certainly in the landscape I've gone from Vermont to Oregon in a week. There has been a deep, contrasting chasm between two generations of gay men, which is striking and disturbing.

I stayed with two gay men in their 60's who met and fell in love 41 years ago. Their love is obvious and their partnership in all things has been a blessing for their professional lives, their community, and all manner of charitable good.

Days later I stayed with friends including a gay man in his 80's. He is in the closet and has had a lifetime of deception. While it may have been obvious to any gay man carefully watching, his family was shocked when he was caught soliciting sex from a cop in a public restroom last year.

There was little mercy for him among some of his friends and family, no understanding that his generation and life among church people in the Mid-west made secrecy a necessity and loneliness his constant burden. He married late in life to a woman heartbroken and disappointed by loses in her own life. She is embittered and carries this with arthritis deforming her hands and feet—a hardening inflexibility of the emotions and a hardening inflexibilty of the joints,—not an uncommon pairing. He is more bowed and carries his shame like a full load of bricks on his back. But nothing is said, as they are Midwest Protestants with a reserve close to their British forbearers.

I felt uncomfortable with him. On the one hand I had worked behind the scenes to push for understanding of his condition when news broke. Now seeing him a year after his court time, his attempt to be overly friendly and enthusiastic at my arrival, puts me off. There is an oozing loneliness that pervades wherever his is.

I felt this loneliness too with the uncle I was named after. As a young man, after I had some gay community and understood his plight, I made sure to always give him a big hug upon greeting and leaving. But initially his loneliness scared me. Here I was again, put off by the vast loneliness of a guy caught in a life of nothing much. His biggest life headline was an arrest and subsequent shame that his secret was no longer secret.

The mercy I had for him was used to help lessen the impact initially with his family and friends during his absence. But now face-to-face months later, I could only be cordial in shared conversation. I am accustomed to pain in others. But his combination of loneliness and shame disturbed me. I had only a brief chance to sense it and then be off. The task of healing all this would be exciting work to do together, but there is not time and no sense of willingness or possibility—witnessing a car accident and then no first aid sought or offered, i.e. hell. Blessings on the many generations of silent people who couldn't tell about their love, their rape, their longing, their lost child, their broken heart because the culture requires silence on the topic.

Maybe I can give up the idea that I talk too much as I am making up for all these others who never got to say who they were and how they felt. I will continue my personal opera to say quite loudly who I am and how it feels and take the consequences as ribbons offered from a species still learning how to live after all this time.

By the way there is no direct route from Missoula to Klamath Falls, but the scenery is gorgeous!

Monday 9/20. Best Travel Day

It was a perfect day today. First—my favorite playlist of personal favorites of Joni Mitchell was restored this morning to my iPod, so my favorite traveling music was available. There was a gorgeous weather. And I only had to drive 250 miles. The young man pumping gas into my car was handsome, longing for a trip like mine to go far away. I drove through desert and then abundant farm fields in south central Oregon. The sky, sun, and clouds were beautiful and lush all day. The landscape was extreme and beautiful and kept changing. I had the best bacon cheese burger at the Burger Queen in Lake Something, Oregon.

I am now happily ensconced in my favorite cousin's home, here to work at his treatment center for young adults, Dragonfly Transitions. Tonight he told me I was one of three adults who mattered most in his growing up life. It's so good to have such love returned. His were the first diapers I ever changed. Now he and his wife have built a center that succeeds in saving lives of young people who are in last ditch efforts. I love talking shop with this cousin—how might so and so be helped? My hands are already getting warm.

Next weekend is the QUIT conference that I've been planning with others for the past year. Finally the time has come!

Yes, it's very dangerous to drive and take photos of the landscape when one is driving near cliffs and scaring yourself and everyone in cars around you, very dangerous. I got some good shots.

Wednesday 9/22. From Dragonfly in Oregon to QUIT in California

Two days at a treatment center for young adults with addictions and other mental health issues, I got my hands on 15 people and taught anti-burnout work to a dozen staff. It has been good to visit a place over the years and watch it grow and the great welcome and anticipation of good things coming help the work to go smoothly.

Mostly the young people needed deep relaxation, a break in their patterns of anxiety and depression. Energy work is surprisingly good for this. Hands-on work with staff was very good. I love working with therapists. They carry a difficult witness, knowing so much intimacy, so many secrets shared. They need a special space to rest and feel only themselves and lay down the intake. Although the details and particulars are different with each person, in general, everyone has pain of some sort and everyone is in need of some extra help. When they slow down enough to have some stillness, they can get more honest. When there is a good possibility of relief in sight, things get better.

Once relief is felt, then some hope may be restored, then more relief can be had, learned, and stocked moving along in life. I am looking for everyone to have a good ride, a better ride. Since we are going on the ride anyway, we might as well make it a good ride. Our lives are the masterpieces of all our efforts. More Light makes for better rides. I'm happy to be a big old queen with this life work. There is much work and much Light. What more might a Quaker want?

In California driving south to fetch Scilla Wahrhaftig of Pittsburgh, Pennsylvania American Friends Service Committee and Chuck Fager of Quaker House in Fayetteville, North Carolina as the workhorses of the steering committee of QUIT—The Quaker Initiative to End Torture. From the airport Thursday afternoon, we go on to Quaker Center in Ben Lomond. After a year of planning, we come together for the 4th QUIT conference.

Sunday 9/26. The 4th QUIT Conference

Thank you for all your notes and for holding the QUIT conference in the Light. The conference was excellent! All four presenters outdid themselves in presenting current information from their fields.

Terry Kupers, author of *Prison Madness*, gave us clear information about how the use of torture in American prisons results in deformed people, unable to live as whole humans.

Father Roy Bourgeois explained the history of the School of the Americas and it's torture training for more than 60,000 Latin American military and police. It continues.

Scott Horton, lawyer and author of *Harper's* magazine "*No Comment*" column, explained the legal context in which Obama not only continues Bush policies, but in some instances makes things worse regarding torture.

Hector Aristizabal, Colombian torture survivor and therapist, showed us how movement and play can help us integrate all three days of information and emotions.

California has good and active groups working against torture and we heard of several actions taken in recent years—everything from clown protests to legislation. Quakers and others from North Carolina, Idaho, and Oregon, along with many Californians, attended.

Tuesday 9/28. Rest and Restoration

Marshall scheduled a vacation to coincide with the QUIT conference and the week following. He brought two cameras and shot all the presentations. We left Ben Lomond to spend two days at the beach. I am quite tired from the travel and work, and the conference is the culmination of hundreds of hours put in over the last 12 months. Now to be with Marshall and suddenly without schedule or public demands is a delight. The Pacific surf pounds in our ears during on the beach and all night long.

Long beach walks are my idea of heaven. Some year I must live at least part of the year where I can take walks each day. To rest in Marshall's arms listening to the surf is a luxury beyond all I ever hoped for. For the level of output I've been doing, it's the balance I need to restore and go on.

Up the coast elephant seals crowd a beach like a parking lot of fat buses. They come to breed in harems. The babies are so beautiful and the old bulls are gigantic, loud, and fierce. Safe in our room we hear continually rolling surf, whose sound is comforting and cleansing all at the same time. We study the houses along the beach to see how more and more light could be let in so that each room has a beach view. Day dreaming about houses on grand sites is a favorite old pastime of mine. We nap a bit and go slowly. We are both restored in this quiet little beach town. Along with being luxurious, this is also spiritual discipline, because it means I can now do more, lots more.

Friday 10/1. A Short Visit in a Nice Town

John Pixley has a sweet little home in one corner of Claremont not far from the Friends Meeting House. Claremont is an ideal Southern California town set up by Ivy League alums from the Northeast. With street names like Yale and Harvard, it's beautiful, well governed, and has five colleges right smack in the center of town, plus a famous theology school. Two large retirement homes are full of clergy, still busy shaking up the world, bending towards justice.

John and I briefly visited the other day, maybe too briefly. John showed me his new talking machine. It looks to be a life-changing tool creating a better bridge between him and others. It seems almost magical that the tiny bit of silver on the bridge of his eye glasses directs a cursor on a computer screen that chooses words or phrases. He now composes sentences and paragraphs with the careful movement of his head. It saves him the effort of clicking one letter at a time on a keyboard, which needed the use of his whole body.

I am only half way good at understanding his speech and when we strike an impasse, John seemed to go still, almost trance like. I soon realize that he was not in prayer for increasing the size of my brain, but rather focusing on getting the word or phrase spoken by his Dynavox. It is a treat and makes me feel giddy to see this liberation of his voice, of his mind. It's a delight to be so happy for another's sudden freedom.

Friday 10/1. Going East to the Southwest

After a few days with Marshall's folks in Southern California, I leave for Arizona. Marshall will fly home and I continue to teach in Tucson, Santa Fe, and Albuquerque. Email has been spotty here—mostly we go to Marshall's sister's house. We took his dad out to see if his failing eyesight might like to use an E-reader as books and newspapers no longer work well. After several stores and machines, he tried an iPad from Apple, which is far and away the best tool for him. As his technology experience is no more than using a flashlight, this is not an easy transition. Marshall did a great job of making it all less foreign.

After a few stores I got bored and wandered around. Marshall's 16 year old nephew wandered with me. He is taller than me and built like a refrigerator. We had a bit of fun when a salesman tried to sell us a Flip video camera. I say this is my grandson. Well, says the salesman, if he does sports, this camera would be great to make movies of his team. Well, does it work inside? Because he'll be doing a ballet concert next weekend. The salesman's surprise, the absurdity of this dump truck-sized fullback in tights, and our bursts of laughter bring the game to a sudden end, but all were laughing. I remind this nephew that he has to learn to lie better so he and Aunt John can have more fun out in the world. Responsibility for young people is serious work and I'm so glad others are doing it.

There is something about long trips that suits me. After the maps have been surveyed for routes, the packing of best things, and the vehicle checked, washed, and readied, the open road engages me in ways I can't explain. Maybe some past life of wandering or being held captive makes for this excitement in me now. I'm about to pack up after a few days and go to the next stop. At least that's the plan—all plans should always be in pencil, of course. The universe is very busy and can't always accommodate one's best schedule, no matter how large a tantrum is thrown.

Driving cross-country lets me see how really big the land is and how much it changes. Coming across the Great Plains I recall the memories in *Black Elk Speaks*. In the Northwest, the thick forests remind me of stories of all the great ships and barns built from trees larger than Europeans knew existed. The shapes of the land, the changes in air and light, how much land there is without human structures reminds me of how it runs on to the horizon free of our infection of civilization.

The richest parts of the trip are the encounters with people. Old friends, strangers, coworkers and collaborators, even the waitress at the diner telling the busboy that his hangover is the result of dumbness and not studly, all are a great show of humanity. In some ways, each day is so rich with people that it's almost like eating too much. One needs to give the mind and belly a day of rest, of fasting. But the next day has its own people and there is no off switch. The loss is mainly that I have no time to ponder or roll about in my affection for so-and-so before a whole new batch of lives comes into focus and contact. It's richness I can live with. But part of me yearns like a painter to halt the loss of sunlight at the end of day, so that I might catch it right before it fades.

I love my cars beyond my understanding. I had the same feeling about my first bicycle. I cleaned it, oiled and tightened the chain, and adjusted the seat and handle bars. I rode the poor thing more hours and days than metal and rubber could bear, but with huge delight and wanting to go farther all the time. Maybe it's the way Roy Rogers loved Trigger. Trigger came when called, broke Roy out of jail, and spent more time with Roy than Dale did- maybe I shouldn't go into that. Roy had an all round good friend, mostly taking him away and back home, over and over.

Each of my cars has felt like more than a purchased machine. They have been more like co-conspirators making plans for some adventure, stepping out and away from the restrictions of civilized society, over-busy schedules, and rebelling against staying in one place. Is all my Attention Deficit Disorder mere Gypsy longing to never be stuck in one place? What makes the car the antidote, the medicine, and relief? What others thought of as mere squirreliness actually needed wandering a whole continent to be calm?

Three VW buses, three Saabs, and an heroic stint by a VW Rabbit has had me on the road since I left home at 18. Oddly, I have gotten to beautiful places and even made a home in a small paradise, but the draw to go is no less after 40 years of packing and going. I can't explain the affection I have for my car. I love that it runs so well, that it's beautiful, that it's safe, and that it takes me so far so comfortably. One loves a tool of one's work and life. But really, this is true love.

Sunday 10/2. Phoenix Tales

Marshall's niece is in college. We go to Arizona and take her out to dinner. The waiter is young, cute, and friendly. I ask her opinion. Yes, he's cute but she's thinking more about her degree. She prefers control and practical, realistic possibilities over flinging herself into adventure. She is tall and beautiful and smart and strong. A good man to match her will not be easy to come by. She'll be a designer in a few years and is a very interesting person with wonderful, creative powers and a family devoid of pathologies- such a deal.

Afterwards we go to Frank Lloyd Wright's Biltmore Hotel to view the beautiful building and have a drink at the bar. The hotel is a stunning work of art and feels gracious just to walk inside. We stroll a bit trying not to look too much like tourists. A drink at the bar is a lovely way to view details and relax after a long trip across the desert. The barmaid asks if we are traveling and before I can stop myself I explain that we three are on our way to LA to buy an old family circus. It has lots of clowns and acrobats, but no animals, since that is too much trouble, all those bales of hay, declawing the tigers, etc. Marshall and niece laugh on the inside but hold the straight faces of conspirators. She joins in and is a pro at spinning the tale. I fill in content much too easily. There's no excuse for this behavior, really. I can tell a good story, but I am not a good liar, too worried about being caught. I'd like to claim I'm moral, but really lousy liars should just stick to telling exaggerated stories and leave deceit to used car salesmen and politicians.

Marshall flew home this morning. I love traveling with him. He's so good at spontaneity. First, I traveled alone for ten days. Then, we had a week together. Now, I see him again near the end of October, our travels crisscrossing. It's always sad to separate. I teach in three more cities on this trip. I make stops to visit more dear old friends and this is always wonderful. I'm 4,000 miles into this trip and have seen more people than I can recall easily. Things begin to blur in my wee mind. Marshall works in Korea next. I'll see him at home for one day before he works on the west coast for three weeks. We'll be done with travel by Thanksgiving.

Sunday 10/3. The Very Big Desert

Pima Meeting in Tucson has a lovely meetinghouse. It's an old brick house that is grand, faces a park, and holds a wonderful meeting doing good works in the world. The people are friendly and I'm always surprised to see old friends transplanted to new places. There's that wonderful experience when I come into a large group of mostly strangers and leave a few days later knowing many names and recognizing the faces of new friends I've come to know via teaching and touching.

Tucson in early October seems to cool down at night into the mid-80's and still heats up to high 90's and more in the day. My first afternoon there, temps went from 106 to 86 during a rainstorm. This Vermont child is melting and sweating like a pig, while the natives don't even notice the 106 temps. They talk about winter gardens planted in January and how silly it is to plant in June, as the new plants can't take the heat. They say the river runs sometimes after a rain and waterfalls are unheard of in these parts.

Mostly it feels foreign, but in a way that intrigues me and makes me want to see more and go further into the desert to feel the miracles of growth and life that seem to come out of rock and sand and the rare rain drop. Both the North and South Poles are more akin to Vermont than this outpost.

I love seeing the very old men and women whose skin has been worn by the desert air into craggy wrinkles and small tight bodies that have no spare water in them. In my mind, it's a desert body type here and the meetinghouse held several of them today as we worked together on both Goodness and Deep Relaxation. I envy their feeling of being solid and comfortable in this desert land. I can imagine visiting here, maybe coming in the winter to write, but living here seems beyond my imagination.

Tomorrow an old friend in Truth or Consequences will welcome me. I'll have a bit of rest before going on to teach in Santa Fe and Albuquerque. This is such a luxury to see so many wonderful people and places. It's a luxury to feel so well used in the ministry. It is a luxury to enjoy the work even though it drags me out of my shyness, which I sense is more original and organic than my in-the-spotlight teacher persona. It's the Light that makes me do it!

Marshall is home and says the October colors are amazing. The fog from the river drifts up the valley in the mornings. We are very grateful that John Meyer stacked the last of the firewood and that the new roof is in place for winter. Our home is so cozy come the first snow, a different world from here, weeks and miles away.

Tuesday 10/5. The Spiritual and the Material

An interesting question during a recent teaching—does the depth of my faith determine the depth in my healing work? Good question. Seems obvious in some ways that the answer should be yes. But, here's what I what I experience. Since the healing is a spiritual gift of grace, it is not in the least dependent on me and my perfection. It is rather the experience of grace moving through me that engages me and strengthens my faith.

My imperfections make me the perfect student for conversion to deep spiritual belief. Better to use the fool who can move into ministry proper than the "holy" man who's already convinced. At heart I am a rascal and bad boy, but the Light is so strong I have to go and see what's there. There are disciplines that have to be learned and followed, as the waters are deep. Being qualified or entirely ready ahead of time is not an accurate look at me. I am better at preparations now, almost 30 years since beginning. But if all success were built on my faith, there would not be a full calendar to show for it each year.

On the more material side, about noon today my right eye suddenly developed spidery lines across it. When I looked in the mirror and saw the external eye was clear, I got a message that I'd burst a blood vessel inside my retina. I stopped into an emergency room off the interstate and was referred to an eye doctor who confirmed my diagnosis. It's normal aging, no sight damage, no pain, will clear itself, more floaters will appear as the blood clears from my vision. I was trying not to be scared and had almost convinced myself. But the doctor's clarity brought great relief and made me very happy. I am not good at suspense. Reading a mystery is out of the question. Not knowing if I had something much more serious going on drained me of energy. But all is well. Travel goes on and I'll be fine after some sleep.

Fear while waiting in the hospital is made less by being in prayer for those around me clearly in more pain and danger than I was. I do so well with other people's stuff. For myself, I'm a complete coward. Thank goodness for cute young doctors who need to be very close to see into one's eye. All distractions welcome. The mercy of a simple diagnosis is an immeasurable relief. Makes me grateful for all life.

On to the next stop, a dear old friend in Truth or Consequences. She makes the best chocolate truffles in the country! We've known each other so long, she's known several of me- the young, gay ,hippie school teacher and now several people later the old married Quaker healer anti-torture crusader. She is talented and adventurous in ways similar to me and in ways very separate. She's mastered many things, while I've polished one stone in the 30 plus years we've known each other. We laugh a lot, mostly at ourselves. It takes a whole evening to remember all the times and places we've come into one another's lives. All of this makes life feel less extreme and slightly more logical.

Wednesday 10/6. Enchanted by Light

I don't know what it is about New Mexico, but I am always so enchanted when I see it again. It causes me to wonder why I don't live here. This has happened on several visits now. Its beauty and feel and light, the spaciousness and landforms all speak to me of some unknown home in time that I recognize.

There was a time yesterday crossing the Arizona-New Mexico border where I was surrounded by flat desert for miles with high mountains in the far distance in all directions- amazing. There was a sense that my home state could be tucked up into one corner for storage.

I arrived in Santa Fe and got lost with the help of maps. This city has lots of roads and few straight lines. I only got a little lost, but for a long time. I had some sense of where I wanted to go, but didn't find it right away. I ended up at the Santa Fe Friends Meeting, where I was graciously let in and given a lovely couch to nap on. I slept about two hours, waking up more awake than I had this morning. Later, I found my lodgings across town.

It is so beautiful here. I-25 takes in much of the view from low and high. One can see all of Albuquerque coming from the south, like some huge, sprawling city gone low and green. And always mountains are in view in more than one direction. The scale and the light combine to create a constant show to engage the mind. I'm in New Mexico for four days and then off to Colorado. The ride up Raton Pass is always a thrill- too thrilling in snow, but I should be safe as a heat wave has been through recently.

Wonderful to get the many good notes of folks enjoying the shorts bits of writing on this trip—much appreciated. I wish I could write the confidential stuff. Would like to describe what it feels like to see obsessive/compulsive disorder leave a young person free for half an hour for the first time in years after a short session of energy work. Would like to say what it felt like to work on the incestuous rapist in his meetinghouse and feel all the self-hatred take a break from crippling his spine. Would like to talk about the torn rotator cuff, the broken heart from the old boyfriend's suicide putting her back out, the gifted young healer who had no idea of such in herself. All this might be recent information or from another year, but is not to be shared because it's confidential. And so I tell you about what I can—a few people but nothing too over the top, how the trip feels, what the land looks like.

But of course as seekers hungry for Light and at the mystical end of Christianity (which is where all the comparative religion books put us), Quakers know that there are other travels going on for all of us—and as my travels are often other people's travels, I can only say so much. I suppose I could do a book of stories and send it out 50 years after I'm gone. But in my heart of hearts I'd love to share it now and sit with you in awe of what Light makes possible even with mere schmoes like me who are the least important part of such transactions. When any person gets even a glimpse that their stone can be rolled away, that's a moment of awe, teaching them healing is possible and the worst doesn't have to stay as it is. Other than that, not much else is new. Weather here is more moderate than in the south.

Friday 10/8. Thrift Store Addiction

I've new levels of madness today for true. When I was packing for this trip, I brought too many clothes. I knew it and couldn't change. So here I am with an overloaded trunk, freshly laundered clothes stuffed in suitcases preparing to go from Santa Fe to Albuquerque and lo—the Goodwill was on the way to lunch! Now I've been hearing about the Santa Fe Goodwill for years—a tad pricey but good stuff and lots of it.

I don't need a thing. I've too much of many things. But nature called, and I was a magnet caught on steel. The only way to compensate was to be extremely picky. Any shirt must fit all criteria completely to be considered for purchase. First, only my colors: blues in medium, slate, and navy not too dark or bright. Red, some greens, bold, and not fine patterns. Second- absolutely only natural fibers. Button-downs preferred. No knits- my tits are too big and I look like a wet nurse pulling overtime. Third- must have no spots, missing buttons, or worn collars or cuffs. Fourth- I have to really love it and not already have two! This makes it a pretty safe bet, even for me. (Marshall says I don't have to go to 12-step if I only buy from thrift stores once a week.)

The navy blue silk shirt was just too wonderful. The heavy hunter green cotton shirt had to come with me too. I love heavy cotton. And the blue Hawaiian cotton was just too fun to leave. Also Woody Allen's book, *Without Feathers*, is good light reading for traveling. I scoured the place like Sherlock Holmes looking for any nice leather bags or wallets—nada, zip, schmatz!

There were some jackets and sweaters that were good buys, fit, and were good materials. But I really didn't need them and the trunk is already overfull. See, I did show some discipline, a little bit. It was a relief. My own madness has some limits, always a nice surprise.

I am staying in a new cohousing group with several buildings and some gardens and a common house with a big kitchen and dining room with a fireplace, an office, and a guest room. I've two friends living here. They are the kind of old Quaker ladies that makes one happy to be getting older. Their lives have been full of adventures and travels. Now somehow, though they are each very different from each other, they both, along with several others in this adventure, are settlers in a new proposition, a very green, shared housing, planned neighborhood, where they decide as a group their culture and lifestyles. I enjoy that they are strong, old, clear of vision without the ambition of youth, and with great care for their impact and intention. It feels very good to be here and to be with them. I do a bit of work in the neighborhood, but mostly I am left to rest, mercifully. I get my hands on one friend who melts into comfort and rests deeply. The lack of touch, the absence of hugs and kisses is a kind of starvation that comes to many older people in sneaky ways and hurts like hell in quiet ways. This must be guarded against. Be generous with hugs, especially with the old. Hold on and make that moment lush.

Santa Fe Friends are wonderful in their welcome and careful listening tonight as I held forth on The Quaker Initiative to End Torture and then Goodness. It was a wonderful group of almost thirty people, good questions and deep seeking. I felt washed in Light as I spoke. I probably said "fuck," too much, which is a sign I am tired. But I did explain ideas well, at least gauging by the feedback. I brought enough humor to teach some serious stuff and enough medium stuff to not be overwhelming. I also received many kudos for the plenary I gave at their yearly meeting five years ago. I feel held, well used, and appropriately tired.

I'm off to Albuquerque tomorrow and the end of scheduled teaching for this trip. I feel it's a great luxury just to be here surrounded by mountains and big sky and wonderful people. I hope New England doesn't feel too small. I'm already have feelings of missing New Mexico.

Monday 10/11. A Beautiful City and a Great Highway North

My time in Albuquerque is wonderful. I am given a guest room that is the kind of room one hopes for. A wall of sliding glass doors looks out across lawn to a pool, not far from the table on the terrace where breakfast is served. Again, I am thinking I should offer my adoption papers immediately. My hosts are gracious and welcoming. I had been hoping to see some of the hot air balloon festival. It happens at extremely early hours. My host says that if the wind is right, they will come over the house. I can't quite picture such a thing, but try to believe her.

The next morning, immediately out of the shower, comes the cal. "Quick! Walk with me to the golf course. The balloons are flying overhead." There we are striding before I'm actually awake toward the more open area of the golf course. Up in the air every so often is a gigantic explosion of color looking more surreal than can be described. Yes, the balloons fly over the houses and quietly seem like elephants or teardrop boulders the size of a small house just floating by like smoke. This is the freakiest thing I've ever seen. It makes me laugh. I wonder what is it like from up there? It's like a circus playing in the air. It's silly and odd and friendly somehow. I wonder about the first person who said, "I know let's fill up a bladder with hot gas and fly on the wind!" To whom could one say this? My host indulges my childlike delight and we stroll back for breakfast. She is a wonderful person to be with and the way she talks about her kids, one can feel she's a good mom.

The Albuquerque Friends Meetinghouse is a lovely building with two walls of windows shining the bright New Mexico sun into the room and a stage along one wall with a piano. Something about a stage in a meeting room makes me feel something large will be revealed, by and by. The people gather slowly on this warm, sunny, day and some come from afar. Some are from the university and others have come in from the desert. As always, seeking is done in various ways with similar hopes.

I spend the first hour teaching about American torture and the work of The Quaker Initiative to End Torture- QUIT! People had some vague sense but didn't really know that American torture began long before George W. Bush and hasn't ended with Barack Obama. Their questions are good. I trust some actions will come of this.

Then I teach about deep relaxation and its importance to a deeper spiritual life. Can we use deep stillness to rest and to be aware? To lay down the noise of popular American culture is important to being open to messages and guidance of Light. I've a few old friends in the crowd and it's good to be with them. One old Quaker lady has a come hither look in her bright blue eyes and I'm sure has numerous stories to tell amidst other stories of loftier seeking. I get my hands on one old friend with serious illness and this is a comfort to both of us as the energy flows with the heat of my hands to her core. Having friends all across country and some of them quite ill means that I long for my touch to reach them. While my heart stretches and reaches like some hound hot on the trail. Now, in the same room, I have the luxury of hands-on and we both bask in the comfort of direct helping in person. One old friend breaks down into weeping from all the sad stories she's heard from work. I hold her and encourage her to weep and be washed in her grief's release and, mostly, she does. Later she looks younger and not so tired and clear as a bell. We do get afraid of letting it go and the burden grows. I can see why opera is so easily done in Italian, where they are used to big voices and big drama, and no emotions are secret, but rather compete in a crowded field. This tradition I know experientially.

Later, my car is rocketing along I-25 going north. I had hoped to get farther, but I am too tired to reach Raton. I do not go as far and am asleep soon after dark. The drive along I-25 is stunning to me at every turn. Especially in northern New Mexico, there are wide, open fields that go on for miles and miles that seemed golden in the afternoon light. Behind them tall pines and beyond them the Rocky Mountains loom higher and higher. This is too beautiful and makes me want to stay.

The long drive north, passing Santa Fe, and leaving New Mexico is a bit sad for me. I know soon I'll turn east and I will miss the drama of the landscape, the very large forms, and the light only New Mexico has. About an hour from Raton Pass along I-25, there are rolling plateaus going off into the distance, golden with hay and edged by higher plateaus of rock and trees. The mountains frame these layers of differing forms, always catching the eye, intriguing.

Scheduled work is now done and the travel is looser. I have work at home awaiting me and there are more visits along the way. But now that teaching/touching work is done, I am feeling the kind of tired you don't allow yourself to feel until after finals in school. I am physically tired and a bit peopled out. I need some solitude and rest alone, time to recover, but none was in the plan. Memo to self- old queens who are itinerant teachers/healers need more time between weeks of work in a row.

I was to stay in Denver with a dear friend, but in truth I'm peopled out. I need some immediate solitude and alone time, without even the kindness of good hospitality of a sweet person asking my favorite foods for breakfast. I drive on to Boulder feeling guilty that I would not see this Denver friend. But I choose rightly, as a grouchy John really is best alone to nap. Refreshment is essential lest anyone see how truly awful I can be. I was here for the largest changes in my life. From 1982 to 1985 I was in massage school and began my work with rape survivors and people with AIDS before we even had that word. It's here that I learned about my spiritual gift to release pain, here I surrendered my life to this blessing, and here I began to live on gifts.

As I drive through town a flood of memories come- faces without names, names without current idea of what's become of them, memories of my own transitions from numb-nuts to a young healer, thrilled and terrified of what would be next. My own healing from lonely, skinny, angry, and horny to empowered in all the same areas. What came was deep friendships, normal body weight with new muscles from doing massage, a better knowledge of the anger I would study for years, and a full dance card!

I have the same feeling for Boulder that people have for their college towns when that time was good. This time of change and growth for me was very good. I was a late bloomer, came of age here at 30, and charted a new life.

I have some fear of turning east. It means leaving the mountains, and by and by it will mean more crowding civilization and all the work that awaits me at home, and finally, winter. Soon, too soon.

I shouldn't be writing the obit of this trip just yet. I won't be home for almost a week. I suppose it's the fatigue of lots of good work and the many miles. It's also that the QUIT conference and this trip took months and months to organize and present. And now these tasks are done. I am feeling full and good and needing a nap before bed.

I've had great delight in seeing so many old friends, and in reaching into the lives of many new people, too. I've seen the country in a way that let's me rejoice in its beauty and take great pleasure in its size. There are only five states I haven't been to and another road trip could take care of that.

Tuesday 10/12. Is This Disaster or Not?

Going into Kansas, the check engine light came on in the evening. The car was running fine but this light was speaking some unknown truth. Having driven across much of beautiful Kansas going slowly as the car insisted, I am now on two days of enforced hotel rest while the car is repaired. I'm happy not to have been stranded and towed off the highway. The repair is free. I can use the time to rest some more after that slow day in Boulder. I am more relieved than anything else.

I will miss seeing an aunt in St Louis. She was going to give me a wood carving by a favorite uncle, who died two years ago. The family asked me to give the eulogy at that time, which was in the same Catholic church where I had First Communion over 50 years ago. I will not be able to see a friend in Ohio, either, as my current placement on the map and driving days to get home are now off kilter from original plans. I want to get home efficiently so that I can really and truly be back. I pack the following Sunday to teach away from home, again!

Things are not always as we plan. The cosmic plan has more authority, in general. I'm going to do some thank you notes tomorrow and make some calls, but generally go slowly. Since I wanted some slow alone time, here it is—although not where I had intended.

Watching the Rocky Mountains disappear in the rearview mirror is sad. The great plains are beautiful, but I've been so taken with the drama of mountains and deserts. The whole east-bound part of this trip is a kind of farewell- to an adventure, to big beautiful landscapes, to the heat of summer, to close friends far away, to the freedom of travel and wonderful work, and people in new places.

In Boulder I spent some time going through the phone book to see if some clients were still alive. The time of AIDS early on meant many missing might be gone away or actually dead. Such memories come with wondering what became of ___And___ And___. Should I look at the AIDS Quilt website for them?

The SAAB service hotline 800# was kind and courteous. But when it comes to helping me get help along I-70, they don't hold a candle to Liz Keeney. She had map, Google, and numbers for me to call in mere moments. The nice SAAB lady couldn't use her computer the way I needed her too. I suggested she ask her boss for a map and paper list of

SAAB mechanics. Meanwhile, Liz also makes cookies—which we all know is the real key to the pearly gates! Oddly, I called her while driving through Wakeeney!

There is an odd box here in the hotel called a TV. I'm going to investigate it and report on its contents. It will be hard to improve my low opinion. I have a hard enough time being open minded about people, let alone colossal productions of numb-nuts ninney-brained foolishness. But I'll take a look.

Wednesday 10/13. Belief and Faith

I am off the computer during rest days. Just wanted to make a note on the material and spiritual worlds intersecting in my slow ride across Kansas yesterday. I've been teaching about the two differing perceptions of *God* that Friends often experience.

One is the Big Daddy God, an old white guy on a cloud with a beard who is the cosmic landlord. He owns everything and is a real grouch. Do not anger him! This is the Old Testament God, a simplistic idea learned in early childhood and the early development of human seeking.

The other perception is when we are in a deeply covered meeting and feel the presence keenly and become aware that the Divine is more than any one concept. It is beyond language and much more pervasive than picturing some guy and not at all about anger or meanness. There's an ocean of Light, which we can rejoin any time. We can let go the noise of popular culture and enter into a flow that is ever present.

And yet when the shit hits the fan, we commonly go running to Big Daddy God to fix it all, forsaking all we know, relinquishing all our power, and abandoning all our experiences of being aspects of the Divine. How might we stop responding like children and take the time to observe as well as we are able? How can we seek understanding and join with the Light to have feelings and wonder in balance? How can we not take it all so personally, as only a child will do, and see a larger picture.

Here's me yesterday driving across Kansas when my car suddenly lost all power and then revives. Things to fear—breaking down, stranded on the interstate; cost of tow and repair; missing visits with dear ones; having to get a dozen of my favorite leather bags home without my own car. This fear takes a toll on me physically, especially after a month of travel work. And the two storms that caught my eye to the NE & NW- was that just rain or tornadoes? Fortunately, I didn't lurch into Oh Please Save Me, Spare Me, Help Me and hand over all my power to the childhood image similar to Michelangelo's painting of God and Adam—talk about an old boys network. Instead, I asked for understanding and patience and wondered what I could know about what I needed just then. Yes, there was a SAAB dealer far from here. Was there one closer? What were the symptoms of the car telling me? Going slower helped a lot. Going sixty, not seventy meant the car kept going and didn't lose power.

The hard part was hours more on the road in the state of fear. I tried not to hand over reverence, seeking, wisdom, and power to fear and hysteria, of which I am so very capable. It was exhausting. It was another experiment/trial in keeping with one's best, and I am slowly better at it each year. The Light gives me calm and understanding and this gives power to our divine connection and makes less use of fear. Wish I had known this better during early childhood violence and adolescence loneliness. It's a good thing life is long. There's so much to figure out and practice.

Thursday 10/14. Wondering

I've had fantasies of living in a hotel for years now. There are romantic stories of writers living in hotels and working while enjoying being anonymous in a city and the luxury of amenities without housework. I can imagine a beautiful room in some lovely place with only writing to be done. That idea has a lot of order and simplicity to it, complexity alleviated. I imagine being productive and single minded and few things going on.

Maybe I've made a life of too much. My home is a bushel of distractions from writing. Even good choices can gather into a heap. Always a dozen undone projects, good ideas left in stacks that nag at me even though I am busy getting some of them done. Are space and time more luxury than I'll ever see? Or just some whining? Is it craving less due to age or wanting more depth in fewer venues?

I remember in the early days of the AIDS epidemic coming home to Boulder from doing massage on dying men in Denver. I'd sit wearily on the back porch and watch the neighbor, Thelma Maydew, who was at least in her 90's, doing the chores around her tidy yard and house. She was always in motion, but in a finite measurable world that was just her own. I envied her simplicity. Is my life such that I've gone waist deep into all I wanted to seek and now feeling a tad too old or tired to be this engaged? I am thinking this is a common feeling among seekers who have the time to wonder about this in their late 50's early 60's. Am I adjusting to another period in life- more mastery, less energy? Am I selfishly wanting more time to write, so I am leaving more behind, wanting to be remembered and thought well of? That's kind of ego silly and kind of true.

What's left behind of a life? My father built our house and now it's crumbling. My mother leaves nothing behind but three boys, each with varying success of making lives they want to live. My mentors built good and great lasting things- books, institutions, university departments. They carry a tone and direction. But mostly they left students who take the mentoring and turn it into beautiful parts of life. It's the making of Light that they share. Can I, who has gone a different path, come back to report some way that helps those who come later?

What are my illusions of self? Acting from the gut and making choices of passion and Light are all one can do. One hopes to learn from all the mistakes. How it all hangs together we'll see later on. Meanwhile, I'm going to do what brings more Light. It seems to have worked well. mostly, thus far.

Today I answered the question—If one has a Krispy Kreme sugar-glazed lemon-cream-filled doughnut after a late lunch, will one need an afternoon nap?

Friday 10/15. On the Road Back

I departed Kansas City with a good working car. The part put in in Montana had to be replaced. Stayed in Terre Haute then drove to Erie. Hope to get home late tomorrow to Putney.

My silk bomber, which is the most excellent shade of purple-blue found in a thrift store, was splashed last night by the tray of juice holding the roast beef at the Mongolian Barbeque. Took a shower with it tonight in

Erie. Hoping for the best. Signs saying Dust Storms May Exist the Next 20 Miles are common in southern Arizona. They are unknown in Vermont.

With the car back to full energy and rocketing along the interstate, I find my mind drifting between two thoughts—the many deep interactions with people during this trip, and the work awaiting me at home. I was especially happy to recall that one of the QUIT speakers, psychiatrist Terry Kupers, said that my description of mental health effects from torture was the most accurate he'd ever heard—overwhelming and underwhelming the senses to the point of deconstructing the personality. A woman broke down into deep grief with help of energy work and finally relaxed enough to let go. The young massage student deeply in love saw how this love makes all his touch work deeper, more powerful. An old friend with serious illness allowed me to demonstrate using her body during a workshop. There were a number of young junkies in Oregon. I could feel that simple contentment was a missed floor of their drug trips up high and down way low.

The work at home looms large. I will get weeks of mail from the post office and sort it out, completely unpack, do laundry and a trip to the cleaners before M gets back from Korea, and call the dears over the line in Greenfield to see when I might get my hands on one as her breathing slows, and plan a QUIT steering committee agenda in seven days.

Will I have to build a fire tomorrow to warm the house? And what kind of gift shall I find for the couple next door who just got married, but don't want things? I feel very blessed that all this work and home life, even when it's too much, is of my choosing, all of it good and worthy of the efforts.

Saturday 10/16. Home

8,476 miles. 33 days. 15 pieces of luggage. It's good to be home. Built a fire in the woodstove, closed a few windows, unloaded the car. Made a grocery list. Most of the autumn color in the Northeast is gone. It will cold tonight. There is a lovely moon. My eyesight has really improved in the last few days. I notice our little house isn't as nice as the homes I've stayed in over the last month. I also notice that it's very difficult to be public for an entire month. But mostly I'm noticing how good it is to work hard and a lot and come home. I feel gratitude.

Thanks for sharing the ride with me.

Section 7

Light Work

John Calvi and Elizabeth Watson shared stories about ministry on October 18, 2002, when Elizabeth, a Quaker feminist theologian, was 88 years old.

John: My dear friend, Elizabeth Watson, and I have been having conversations for a long time about doing ministry, about being called to do work. I have always so enjoyed asking her questions and listening to her experience that I thought it might be nice for other people to hear also. I proposed to her that we develop five questions that we could both talk about in our experience of following a leading and working in the Light. We have come up with some questions. I'm John Calvi, and I flew in last night from Vermont. And on the way I made some notes so Elizabeth wouldn't think I was cheating from her answers.

Elisabeth: Now why can't I talk about you?

J: All right, now you can talk about me.

E: I said this morning that I first became aware of John when we were at a conference together and John sang a beautiful song; he had written the words and the music. I had heard that he was into this healing stuff. My first reaction was why doesn't he stick to making beautiful songs and write more beautiful songs and forget all this stuff. I had been a Bible student most of my life, but when I came to the healing miracles in the Gospels, I always hung back and thought too bad they didn't live in the time when we have modern knowledge about illness and cures and medicine. So when John sang his beautiful song I thought "Why doesn't he just stick to singing?"

We were at a conference, we seem to go to the same conference every year, and about three years later at that conference I was taken quite ill and was led into an adjoining room to lie down. Then someone brought John and his healing hands were laid on me and I felt my pain disappear.

I know his gift is genuine because I have experienced it. But he also has given me back a part of the scriptures, because now I know how Jesus healed. He doesn't like the comparison. His initials, you'll note, are JC.

J: I'm in enough trouble Elizabeth.

E: At any rate, we've been good and close friends for many years, and it's always a joy when he comes out this way since I can't travel anymore.

Question 1

What moments do you recall in your early life when you received spiritual direction to guide your life?

E: This is an easy one for me; the answer is "I was seven years old." I grew up in a suburb of Cleveland, across the street from my husband, but at that point we weren't interested in each other. My mother's father was a Methodist minister who had gone out to South Dakota as a circuit rider at a time when it was still a territory. He got on his horse and went around to little settlements all over the eastern part of South Dakota. If someone needed burying, he did it. If someone needed marrying, he did it. Otherwise, he conducted services, counseled with people, and so on.

Well, the summer that I was seven, my mother became worried about her parents. She realized from telephone calls that her father was not well. The Methodist Church, at least in South Dakota, had no pensions, no provisions for any place for him to go. She took my brother and me out there at the beginning of the summer so she could help her parents plan what to do.

Back in our big suburb, I had to go to church and listen to a forty-minute sermon. My brother sat on one side of my father and I on the other, and my father made origami nested boxes for us. Out there in South Dakota I had to go to church too, but it was different. It was exciting! My grandfather usually began the sermon period by telling a Bible story. Only he acted it out, and had different voices for the different parts. He made the whole thing come alive. Later on when he prayed, I knew God was right there listening. When he began his sermon, when he made a special point, the people in the congregation would shout, "AMEN!" And I could hardly wait for those moments so I could shout, "AMEN!"

One train a day came through this little town and paused long enough to bring the mail. When my grandfather wasn't busy, he would walk to the station to see the train come in and pick up the mail, and often I walked with him. One day we were walking along and I asked him a question that was bugging me: "Grampa, how did you get to be a preacher?" And he answered very simply, "God called me."

Well, I thought about this for a moment and I finally asked, "Do you think God would call me to be a preacher too?" And bless his heart, he didn't say God doesn't call girls to be preachers, he told me that God sometimes calls children. He told me about Samuel who lay in bed at night and said, "Speak Lord, for thy servant heareth." He taught me to say that, and that summer when I was seven, every night when I went to bed, I prayed, "Speak Lord, for thy servant heareth."

And by the end of that summer, I came to believe that God had called me to be a preacher like my Grampa. This took hold of my life. It not only affected my interior life, but my outer life as well, and from then on I went straight for the ministry.

The Methodist Church didn't ordain women until 1952, which was long after my time. But I learned that the Congregational Church had never had a bar to ordaining women, so after I finished college I went to Chicago Theological Seminary.

There were more than one hundred men in CTS and ten women, eight of them in the program for religious education; I was one of two in the theological program. I was in class after class where I was the only woman, but I never was made to feel an outsider.

Now, how about you?

J: I asked members of my family whether they had any recollection of me doing anything like healing earlier in my life. My cousin, Rosemary, said, "Oh yes. When you were about five years old and I was, let's see, then eight years old, we were playing on Grandmother's farm, and we fell into a patch of what we called 'itch-weed' - the adults called it nettles - and it was stinging our skin." She said I took us all down to a brook and we put mud on the places that were stinging, and then we washed the mud off in the cold water. She said, "You took the sap from the Jewel Weed and put it on our skin and it stopped hurting completely."

E: And you were what? Five years old?

J: Yes, five. Now, I don't know how I knew such a thing, but once she told me the story, I remembered it.

I think there was a much larger change for me later on. After I had been a schoolteacher for about ten years, I began doing massage. While I was learning massage, the AIDS epidemic came along. Of course, in the beginning we knew so little, and people were dying so quickly; it was a very scary time. But with the very first person I worked on, my hands got so warm that my palms began to peel, and I felt a huge tenderness come over me. It was almost like falling in love, but even more fierce. A fellow who was covered with cancer and terrified and in pain and not able to sleep lost all of his fear, and he lost his pain, and went into a deep sleep. I didn't change his disease state, but he no longer hurt, and that is when I was understood that my work was really beginning.

Question 2

Looking back, what surprised you most about where your work has taken you?

E: It seemed like things I planned did not work out, but something else came along that was better. The first time I remember that specifically was through politics. In the political science department at the University of Chicago, George lost his fellowship. I was in school too, and I decided I had to go to work because I thought it was important for him to finish his degree. I went back to the seminary and talked to the man there about quitting, and he said "If I were in your position, I would take the classified directory and look under settlement houses, and start calling down the list of settlement houses to see if there was a job, because you would get your living out of it as well as some salary."

The first one I called was a place called Association House. The head resident came to the phone when I asked for him, and after awhile he asked me the question, "What's new in theology?" I'm not going to tell you what I answered, but at any rate, after forty minutes, he said, "I guess I ought to meet you before I hire you." So George's losing his fellowship resulted in our going to Association House to live while he wrote his dissertation. Friendships made there and the connection with that wonderful man, who became one of the important people in our lives, are priceless. What we would have missed if George hadn't lost his fellowship! We would have stayed on doing what we were doing.

It always seems that when I plan things to go a certain way and they don't work out, what does happen is something that in retrospect I would . . .

For instance, when we went to Friends World College, George and I had always thought we would like to do a job together, our gifts are very different, and we thought Friends World College would be the ideal place to do it. But they already had a three-person presidency, and they were not interested in having one of the troika be a two-person. So, I didn't get the job; George got the job. I came to know one of the board members who lived there. She worked at Walt Whitman's birthplace. Walt Whitman was born at Huntington on Long Island, where the college headquarters were. When her husband took a job out of town she simply went to the board and said, "I know someone who could do this job." Out of the blue I got a phone call saying, "Would you like to be curator of Walt Whitman's birthplace?" So, one of the most wonderful jobs in the world came to me, and I had not even known it was available. One more example and then I'll turn it over to you.

I made a speech at Illinois Yearly Meeting and Ron Matson, who was known to many of us here, later sent a copy of it to the editor of *Friends Journal*, at that time a man named Jim Lenhart. Out of the blue - I didn't even know Ron Matson had sent a copy of my speech to the yearly meeting - I got a letter from the editor of *Friends Journal*, which started out, "Yesterday I had never heard of you. Now you are one of the most important people in my life. I want to open the pages of the Friends Journal to you. Write for us." Jim later edited *Guests of My Life* and became one of the seminal folks in my writing career.

What has surprised me most is the things that have come when I wasn't seeking them, the opportunities I would have missed if things worked out as I had planned them.

J: It was very much the same for me. Clearly we were not in charge. We didn't know how the schedule was running and decisions were being made somewhere else, and it was always an amazing surprise.

I think about when I was a schoolteacher and how I was pretty much a homebody, and really wasn't interested in travel. I really wasn't interested in meeting people who were very different from me. After about a year where all of my massage work had been trauma work and seeing pain being released out of people's bodies, I really wanted to go and see how many different kinds of trouble I could see and be of help to.

The first large work that I did was to work with women who had been sexually assaulted. And then the next large work I did was to work in the AIDS epidemic. Then I began doing lots of work with refugees who had been tortured. Then I did work in prisons, with people who had had ritual abuse; lots of different kinds of hurt. During this whole time I was receiving invitations to teach about this work, and so, instead of being a shy, quiet person who stays at home, I was getting on the road teaching maybe 24 times a year, sometimes 2,000 people a year. And you know, whether it's going into a prison, or talking at a conference of a thousand people, it's not what a shy person wants. I would walk into the prison and think, How did I get in here? How has this happened? But always, when I began the work of teaching or the work of touching, the Light would become so bright that I would stop feeling foreign no matter where I was, and I would feel the common humanity of everyone I was with. I have been able to go and do that work. I think that's the greatest surprise for me, that I can be doing something so outward. Which is not my original nature; at least I didn't think it was.

Question 3

What has been the most difficult spiritual lesson?

E: That what works in one situation, doesn't necessarily work in another. Let me speak specifically of our first daughter. Sara and I were very much on the same wave length. If there was something she wanted or she wanted the family to do that we couldn't do, I had only to sit down and explain it to her in words that she could understand why we couldn't do that, and it was fine. I thought, There's nothing to raising children. You just talk to them one on one and explain things and that's it. Raising children is a breeze.

Well! Along comes our second daughter, Jean. I would explain to her why she couldn't do something, and I can still see little three-year-old Jean with her hands on her hips, looking up at me and saying, "How can you be sure?" That was her favorite phrase: "How can you be sure?" So what worked with Sara didn't work with Jean. What I learned from that is that everyone, every situation, is new, and that you must try not to carry over what worked in a previous situation, but come into that new situation open to possibilities, and not with a preconceived notion of what's going to work here.

This was a very hard thing for me to learn because, my husband will tell you, I have strong opinions about things. It's one that I'm still working on. Each situation is new, full of possibilities, and I go into it without preconceived notions of how I am going to deal with it. I may have things I want to try, but in my case they usually don't work. But the situation itself produces the appropriate response if I give myself a chance.

Let me just give one example. I've been a public speaker most of my life.

Over many years, occasionally, I would have a failure. I would lose an audience - it was awful. I never could understand why, I never could understand what I had done differently in that situation. At the University of Chicago, the seminarians were required to give a sermon with a few people and faculty members standing around and we all had to take public speaking courses. I took a course, having taken courses on public speaking from junior high on, I finally get the man who could tell me what the situation demanded. When you say something to an audience, you visualize it in your head. You can't be thinking about something else and expect your words to carry it. You visualize it with every ounce of your being; give yourself to it. You don't misfire when that happens.

J: One of the things I am constantly aware of is that there are just so many ways in spiritual work where one has to rearrange oneself. I think the first most difficult things for me were surrender and trust.

As a young person who grew up amidst a lot of violence, trusting other people and letting other people be in charge was not something I was easy with. But when you offer yourself as a conduit for a spiritual gift, your primary job is to let go, to stay tender. I found myself in the peculiar situation of listening to the stories of people's hurts, and finding the discipline to not take these stories deeply into myself, to not relate to them too closely, to not join that other person's suffering. To hear it closely enough that I could be with them as they hurt and then make a contribution to their understanding or to seeing that the feelings in their body could shift in a way that I was not in charge of, that I wasn't steering.

Surrender and trust really was the first part. Then, the awareness of how much I needed to rest was very strange to me. When I first found Quakers when I was 16, there was a wonderful old Quaker lady who said "We should have meeting for worship every day." And I thought, Oh my God, how are we going to save the world when we're sitting in the quiet all the time. There is so much to get done. By and by I understood how correct she was, that having that regular quiet and stillness, and gathering spiritual guidance each day, and resting the body completely, are needed so that you can focus on giving your best for the long haul. Not doing the MOST every day. This was very hard for me to accept. It took much more patience than I had. It's something I still work on.

All of the work with things that you don't know the answer to, working with pain that can't be released, hearing a sad story you know is going to continue. When I was working with refugees, I became accustomed to the story that this person was losing their sanctuary and being sent back to where they would most likely be attacked by the army. When working with people with AIDS, it was very common for me to come to love someone dearly and know them very well, and then help them to die. There is so much that we don't know, so much that there isn't a way of knowing completely. I had to learn to be with it amidst all the unknowing.

Probably the hardest part of all of this is the self-discipline to create the distinction between pride and delight. I really can't take pride that pain is released- it's not really me doing it. But I am the one who makes sure I'm rested and who shows up on time, and who works very hard not to be frightened of the stories I hear. I take great delight in this happening. That delight can feel very close to pride, and I have to be sure that the two don't get confused.

Question 4.

How has marriage enhanced your spiritual work?

E: Growing up with a calling to the ministry, I decided that I wouldn't ever get married, because I couldn't quite see what my husband would be doing while I was being a minister of a church.

Eventually, physiology takes over, and I came to a certain age, and yes, I began to date. George and I grew up on the same street. He is almost two years younger than I am and our families were both active in the Methodist Church. Our parents were part of the same social circle. We grew up together in Lakeland, Ohio, a suburb of Cleveland. Largely through the action of the assistant principal, who was a graduate of Miami University in Oxford, Ohio, we both went there for college. It was possible to go to Miami in Ohio, a state university, for less money than to stay at home and go to Western Reserve.

I went to Oxford, Ohio, to begin college. I will tell you, for reasons that I'm not going to go into, I never had a date while I was in high school. Well, that physiology thing took over when I went to Oxford. Oxford is one of the most beautiful places in the universe. My mother thought I ought to go to Ohio Wesleyan, which was a Methodist college. When we were looking at colleges, I never saw such a drab, uninteresting campus. I had written ahead that we were coming, and when we went into the office, they said, "Well, you just go ahead and look around." We went on to Miami, a state university, and I had written a letter to them as well. They provided a good-looking young man to show us around the campus and to talk about all the opportunities there were, and even my mother said, "I think you ought to go to Miami." She had really felt that going to a state university was not what she wanted me to do but in the light of that experience she changed her mind.

George was a year behind me in school and for much the same reasons, the same assistant principal steering him, and his mother having heard from my mother that I was having a good time there, George, too, came to Miami. He has always been shorter than me and, while I knew he was on campus, we would say hi but that was about it. I met a man at the freshman mixer, and we dated, went steady, and finally after about a year of it I realized he was getting serious, and I took a long look at what it would be to marry a man who wasn't as smart as I was and I broke it off. For a while I wasn't dating because everybody thought I was in a long-term relationship. I was sitting at my desk on a Saturday night working on a term paper, and a gal came down the hall and stuck her head in, "You got a date tonight?" "No." "Well, get dressed." "What do you mean get dressed?" "Well, my date's roommate's date had to go home suddenly, and they have tickets to the dance." During the depression, walking was the main date; you walked. A big date was nursing a 5-cent Coke in a parlor uptown for a whole evening. I've never been able to face a Coke since.

At any rate I said, "Who is it?" and she said "I don't know, but they have tickets for the dance." I get myself all dressed up and go downstairs, and it's George Watson - whom I've known all my life. What's romantic about George? Poor George. He's sitting here suffering through this. At any rate, there was nothing to do but go on to the dance. . .

We applied for graduate fellowships at all the same places when we graduated from Miami, but we got them in two different places. I was at Chicago, George was at the University of Illinois, a hundred and twenty miles down the Illinois Central Railroad. I was in the seminary with over a hundred men and ten women, eight of them in religious education. In class after class I was the only woman. George kept the Illinois Central Railroad busy.

Well, we were married then. Our families insisted that we be married by the Methodist minister, but I did not want to have a big wedding, so we were married in my home with the Methodist minister and a few family members.

Then we went back to Chicago to do our graduate work. World War II was looming on the horizon and the Methodist Church where we had grown up had taught us both that war was wrong. But now, with the Second World War coming along, the Methodist Church backtracked and said this is a "just war." George and I said to each other, we need to find some spiritual home that believes war is wrong even when there's a war on. The only thing we knew about Quakers was that that was true of them. We went to the Friends Meeting, which was very close to the campus. I had preached all through college at little churches that couldn't afford a minister, and I think one of the things I loved to do most was write liturgy. I loved creating a service of worship where everything leads up to what I was going to sock it to them with in the sermon, and wind it down with a hymn and with an appropriate benediction.

We went to 57th Street Meeting and walked into a room of people sitting with no one at the head. It was a long, narrow room. We found a place to sit down, and it was a gathered meeting that morning. After about 15 minutes, one person spoke, and I think two more people spoke after that, each one carrying the thought further. The last one summarized it all. And I was shaken. I thought I was very good at programming other people's worship, but how much better to have worship arising out of the group, with no one, human at least, programming it!

George went boldly up to somebody and said, "How do we join?" They said, well here, you'd better read something first. We went home with stuff to read after having been invited to dinner. By the time we joined Friends, four months later, they knew us, we knew them. And in many ways 57th Street Meeting, which we belonged to for 35 years, which had memorial services for us, and all kinds of things, seems like our spiritual home. That was true at the time. We have also belonged to two smaller meetings; one on the campus at Friends World College, and I'm glad to say that I feel that Minneapolis Meeting, for a large city meeting, is very much a beloved community, and I'm grateful to belong there and to be part of it.

Quakerism, then, has underlain our marriage. We began our marriage - I was still at seminary at the time - with questions about what we could honestly ask each other. What can we honestly believe intellectually? For much of the first year of our marriage we were talking about that. What could we honestly believe without compromising our intellects?

So, Quakerism has underlain our marriage. I've been so grateful that we found it together, that we found it at the beginning of our marriage. We've belonged to four meetings now in our 65 years of marriage - two small, two big. I don't think Minneapolis Meeting is "too big." I think it's wonderful. I love it.

Beyond that, marriage has provided me with someone who is always there for me when I'm at my most difficult. I've never doubted that he loved me. I think that's enough.

JC: How wonderful! 65 years! George, you are a strong man.

I remember a time early in my work when I was still learning to accept that I had a spiritual gift and there came a moment one day when I got a very clear spiritual message, "You are never working alone. It is never just you. We're always by your side. We're always guiding you, and you are never alone."

It was such a strong and clear message, I remember becoming very teary, and feeling very tender hearted all the rest of the day. I understood that I could do any work that was brought to me because of that.

About two years later, here comes a wonderful man who essentially said the same thing. I can see all of you, I love all of you, and I understand how important the work is. And so I will make a pledge to take jobs that will make it possible for you to continue your work no matter where it leads. I thought, Oh my goodness! This is, this is an awful lot. This is a fellow who had a Methodist preacher grandfather and was a certified sex educator in the Methodist Church, and after we'd been together for a short while, I also found out that his grandmother was a birthright Friend from Iowa, and that he actually had Mary Dyer and Susan B. Anthony in his family tree. I had someone who understood the importance of doing good work in the world and in helping people and that was part of his tradition also. I think more specifically, I married someone who is tender and sweet, and that has helped me learn how to be more tender myself.

I came with all of the strength needed to do my work. I've got plenty of extra strength, most of it under the category of stubborn. (I know you don't know anything about that, Elizabeth.) I needed to learn more in the way of trust and surrender and tenderness, and some of that has come from work, but a great deal of it has come from my marriage. I have married someone who is so tender... the other day one of our best friends heard that someone didn't like Marshall, and he said, "Not like Marshall; that's like not liking the Easter bunny." He is so sweet. I think to have the experience of knowing that no matter what happens, no matter what misunderstanding there is, no matter what crises befall us, that there is love no matter what. It was a tremendous surprise for me. This is something for which I am eternally grateful.

Question 5

How has your calling changed or been understood differently over time?

E: As I have indicated, the call came to me at seven, in relatively narrow terms; a call to preach, a call to the ministry.

The summer I was 14, my church sent me to a conference center in Lakeside, Ohio. If any of you are Methodist you may have heard of Lakeside.

A woman there was the wife of the Methodist bishop of India. He was a missionary, an American, and he had just resigned. The reason he gave was that he thought it was now time for the Methodist bishop of India to be an Indian.

But Mrs. Fisher was much more candid. They had met Mohandas Gandhi and become aware that they could no longer try to convert Hindus to Christianity, when Hinduism had produced a more Christ-like person than any Christian they knew. She was full of Gandhi. On the last morning there was some free time and I went to the hotel where she was staying at Lakeside. I boldly went up to the desk and asked if could I speak to Mrs. Fisher. They called up to her room and told her there's a young woman down here who would like to talk to you. She came down and sat on the porch with me for two hours while I asked questions about Gandhi. When she had answered all my questions very fully, she recommended things for me to read and promised to keep in touch with me, which she did for many years.

I came home from the conference and, full of Gandhi, I said, "I hope I can go to India sometime and become a follower of Gandhi." Gandhi was important to me at that point because Gandhi proved that the teachings of Jesus were workable on a large scale in the modern world. My mother quickly said - I don't know if you have sensed that my mother has never quite approved of me and that my father was the go-between - she said, "You can't go be a follower of Gandhi. He's not even a Christian."

My father intervened and said, "You know, you don't have to go to India to be a follower of Gandhi. You can be a follower of Gandhi wherever you are."

At the age of 14 I committed myself to nonviolence, to be a follower of Gandhi wherever and whatever I was doing.

I still had my calling to the ministry that took me to the theological seminary. I had also gotten over my scruples that I was going to be single all my life.

When I went to Chicago Theological Seminary I thought this is a year I can get through until George and I can get married. This was during the Hutchins era. Robert Maynard Hutchins was the fifth president of the University of Chicago. It was one of the most exciting places in the world. What I learned that year was that if something happened to George or something happened to our relationship it would not be the end of the world. There was a great, wide, wonderful world out there to be lived in and explored fully, hopefully with George, but with or without him, life was still going to be exciting. That certainly was one of the most eye-opening, exciting years of my life. George and I were married at the end of my first year. I'm glad I had that year of separation.

I don't know if any of you are into theology, but I was studying under Henry Nelson Wieman, who was the original Process theologian. He invited a few of us to come to his house for what we called a study group. Every week I went to his house where he, in humility with the rest of us, talked about our search for God. Quite late in his life he sent me an inscribed copy of his last book. I had made a friend of him, and I learned Process Theology. It has been the basis for which - I can't say I believe what I believed 65 years ago - but Process Theology has been something on which I could build without ever having to reject it.

I had thought I wanted to go to Union (Theology School), and if I had studied with Reinhold Niebuhr, I don't think I could have lived with his theology all the rest of my life in the way that I've been able to live with Process Theology.

George and I found Quakerism together our first year when we were looking for something that believed that war was wrong even when there was a war on. Quakerism opened many possibilities for ministries for me beyond what I could have imagined. I can only be grateful that we found it at the beginning of our lives and that we found it together.

Now, in old age - I'm 88 - I've had to quit traveling. Three years ago I went into the hospital in Philadelphia where I had gone to make a speech, which I never got to make, having had a heart attack. I was in the hospital in Philadelphia and George was out here in Minnesota. When I got home, my doctor said, "You're not traveling, you're staying home." I haven't been in a hospital since.

How has my calling changed? What's open to me now is to write. I have four more books in my head; whether I'm going to live long enough to get them all written, I don't know. But that's how my calling has changed over the years. It brings me up to my old age with the sense of gratitude that the call came early in life, that it was able to shift as I needed it to shift, and has underlain my life, and my marriage.

I can't tell you how much I love the Society of Friends, and feel so grateful that I was called there rather than going on to be a preacher on my own.

J: We're glad you came along.

As I consider this question I realize what a silly person I am, and how having only a high school education and wanting a good solid job description, I was disappointed most of the time. I was being told at a spiritual level, go over here and look at this and see what you can find out. When I first became a schoolteacher, I thought, this is what I'm going to do for the rest of my life. I'm going to start my own school. I'll have a Montessori school. Then, when I began doing massage, I thought, well now I'm going to start a massage school, and then I thought well, I'm working in the AIDS epidemic, I'm going to figure out how to stop people from dying, and I'll have a school teaching people how to not die. I was always looking to make a specific, particular, concrete idea come along.

I needed to make myself feel safe in a realm that had a lot of pieces and a lot of unknowns. What has changed for me over the years is that all of my definitions, all of my understandings and assumptions of myself, and of the work, and of spiritual life have all become more broad. They've all become gentler.

It seems to me that I am always trying to increase the depth and quality of my spiritual life, but then I realize it's something that can't be pushed. I am very much drawn to a pattern where there is great intensity and then there is great quiet. I love to go and teach in a place where there's a great deal of trouble, to spend a week at a conference where there are two dozen rape survivors, to work with a group of prisoners, helping them learn massage in the context of their prison. Then I step outside of that context and go back to my little house in the woods in Vermont with Marshall and have absolute quiet and stillness and no work. I like those extremes. I like the rhythm of them.

The other thing that has changed over time was that originally, I had a very male, arrogant, prerogative idea that the sainted teacher healer was going to come into the room, and make changes, and teach things that people didn't know, because I had figured it out.

My God! How fabulous! What I came to understand was that all of the healing I needed for my life, as someone who was raped and beaten as a young child, as someone who grew up amidst alcoholism and violence, that all of the healing I needed lay within the context of my work helping other people with their pain. I had a clear spiritual and professional obligation to attend to my own healing first and foremost, and to use everything I was learning for other people's healing. One work always feeds the other and there is always a back and forth wisdom that I can count on. In some ways, it's just gotten much more gentle.

~ ~ ~ ~

J: Now I think, if we still have energy, we might take some questions from the crowd.

Q: Elizabeth, I don't know you very well, and I'm interested in hearing some of the shape and flavors of your ministry, you know, between the ages of 30 and 75. I mean, I'm aware of some of the things - your love for Emily Dickinson - but I'm quite unaware of the various ways you've served.

E: Sometimes, as I said, jobs came to me unlooked for, like working at Walt Whitman's birthplace. You may wonder how my ministry fitted there. There were two of us who had the title curator so we could keep the building open more hours than one person could, more than 40 hours a week. There were often times when I was there alone on a morning. Walt Whitman was gay and he wrote about it openly, in his poetry and more specifically in his prose. His book was banned from libraries and he really was writing for the future because he couldn't get the book published. He actually went down and borrowed a friend's printing press and set the type for the first edition of Leaves of Grass.

There were times when I was out at the birthplace, alone on a weekday morning, and I would see, walking up the path, a young man with the look of someone coming to a shrine. I never said to him, "Aha! I know you are gay." But I got out all the treasures. I did everything I could to let Whitman speak to him, through me, to authenticate that person. Only once did someone tell me that he was gay, but I could often tell from the way they were coming to the house. I felt that this was a ministry, that I could make Walt Whitman available to them, to authenticate who they were.

I think about the world at the present time, and am working on a book on Whitman. Walt Whitman speaks to our time. I have set up file folders with each of the major problems, globalization, HIV AIDS, race relations, whatever. I have this whole set of file folders, and I go through Leaves of Grass, literally page by page and pick out what fits where. I'm hoping to write a book outlining the major problems of our time and what Whitman had to say about them. It's astonishing. He was not accepted in his own times. He was writing for us. "And you that shall cross from shore to shore" - the Brooklyn Bridge wasn't built yet - "Two hundred years from now, you are more in my thoughts than you may think, just as you view this and that, so did I. Just as you walked the streets of Manhattan, I walked the streets of Manhattan." It goes on and on and on. That's my immediate project. I've had various jobs, and I didn't know when I went to the birthplace that a ministry to gay young men would open up for me - my making Whitman available to them.

J: Tell us a little bit more about the other book you would like to write. I would love to hear that.

I wrote *Wisdom's Daughters*, about women in the New Testament. I came to see that more than half those women don't have names. There is the woman with an issue of blood, and that kind of thing. I read whatever was available in the Bible and I tried not to read the other commentaries, but to live with that woman until she revealed her story to me.

Earlier I had written a book but I went to press too soon because I was pressured into doing it, on nine Old Testament women. The next thing that I want to do is to revisit that book, and fill it out. There are nine women there and I want to make it 18 or 19, and rewrite the ones that I've done because I've lived myself more deeply into the lives of those women.

Beyond that, as I have talked to the few cousins I have living, only one on my father's side, only three on my mother's side, we have realized that I know a lot more about our family history than they do. They are pressuring me to write a family history. I'm not necessarily planning to publish that, but I think that while I am still alive, I need to write down what I know about the family history on both sides. As my father said, I'm typically American. On my mother's side I am descended from people who came over to the founding of Jamestown in 1610; on my father's side I was a child of immigrants. And so he said, you are typically American - you're from the first who came here and you're also from recent immigrants. So I want to get that down. And, as I say, I'm being pressured from my cousins to do that while I'm still alive, because they want to pass it on to their children.

J: Other questions?

Q: Actually, this isn't a question.

It's something else that I wanted to say about Elizabeth and her work. I have attended many Friends General Conference Gatherings and heard her afternoon teachings on many topics over the years. I think another dimension of your work that has touched me is your earth-centered theology - bringing the need to preserve our world into a spiritual context, thinking of the earth as our mother and all the ramifications of that. If we really loved God, loved the earth, loved our mother, we would act accordingly. And, I don't know, there's a lot more I could say. I didn't hear that part of your work.

E: You're absolutely right. I see the circle always enlarging. I used to think in terms of race relations in the United States. That's what I went into after I left the seminary. I worked in race relations in Chicago.

Then we went to Friends World College and I was opened up to the world. We were blessed to be able to travel a great deal in other parts of the world, but now, as I am living on borrowed time, I am aware that I am not only related to the people on the planet, I am related to the whole living planet - all of the living things on it, all of the things that are not living on it. I go out at night and look up at the stars, and realize I am part of an incredibly infinite universe. And belonging to all of that is an incredible gift.

Q: My question is a little complicated. For most of my life I didn't think I needed healing. I wanted spiritual growth. I thought, well, I'm a normal person, I'm not traumatized, but I would like to grow spiritually. I was aware that in the Bible Jesus was very involved in healing, but I want to ask you how you see the connection. I'm now moving toward the idea that they are closely connected and I probably need more healing than I realize, but what about people who are not traumatized or in pain, but want to grow spiritually. Do you have any sense of that?

J: I think the opportunity for getting in trouble is always at hand. I'm not at all convinced that there has to be suffering in order for there to be spiritual growth, that there has to be pain or trauma, or a life wound for there to be growth. I do know that when there is trouble, sometimes it will bring out the best in people, sometimes it will bring out the worst in people.

If we're careful and we attend to our spiritual life, when we come to a time of trouble we can treat it as a time of learning. If we are careful and we do the homework well, we can turn the pain and suffering into wisdom and knowledge. The opportunity for very deep seeking is very present when there is great pain. I have surrounded myself so completely with different kinds of hurt that I think the most honest and simple answer I can give to your question is I don't know really. I don't know. I certainly have seen how people can witness the slaughter of their families and still understand that life is beautiful, that some can feel decades of chronic pain and still love life. And I'm simply not too sure about what's happening at the other end of the spectrum.

Q: I want to ask you, John, about your practice as a healer. What do you think stops you, or stops anybody who does healing work, from being able to cure the disease, as opposed to just stopping the pain? Is it the power of the healer, or is it the belief or the non-belief of the healer or the one who's being healed that prevents this from being done? I tend to believe that if the miracles in the Bible are true and that, now, if something needs to be done, it's only a matter of our mind refuses to believe that such a miracle is possible.

If I have a sore throat, it would be okay for me to believe that if I met a doctor by chance in some kind of cafe who wrote me a prescription, and I was out of town and I didn't have doctor, that it was a miracle that I got antibiotics and was cured. Rather than thinking that I'm going to be healed or I'm going to be relieved from that. I don't know.

J: I think that's a very good question, and it's one that I ponder. I don't actually have a clear answer to this question. I certainly have seen and worked with healers who do change physical tissue. I have worked with one or two people who said that I changed their physical tissue or that the Light changed their tissue when I worked with them. I don't know why there seem to be limits at times and not other times. The only thing I understand is that all of our gifts are very individual and very different. I seem to have very sensitive radar to emotional pain. Healing emotional pain resulting from trauma tends to be the place where I can do my best work. In places where there is primarily physical pain, I seem to be good, but not quite as good.

Is that the choices of angels that I have a gift that sings a particular song but not another song? Maybe that's one way to explain it. Is it a limitation in my own experience and understanding, my lack of discipline? Goodness knows that's possible. For me, all of that is speculation. For instance, I've talked with people who've had psychic surgery, where the healer reaches in through the skin and removes the disease and throws it in a cup on the floor. The only thing I can think is that our gifts are as different as our voices. I have one particular stone that I'm carrying and my job is to polish that stone, as obediently and faithfully as I can, and to use the Light from that stone as well as I'm able. Yes. Would it be fabulous to change disease? Absolutely. Would it change my life and my work in a way that I probably would have less grace and wisdom? Absolutely.

I've been doing this work for 20 years. I'm 50 years old, and I think I'm just now getting easy with it. So if they have plans on changing things for me, I would like everyone to go slowly.

Q: Would either of you speak, or each of you speak, to the role of mentors or mentorship in your life in recognizing your gifts, and delivering your gifts, and carrying out your ministry?

J: Along the way I met a healer whose gift was very different from mine. Her gift was being able to look into the body like looking into a milk bottle. Jean Schweitzer could look through your boot and tell you where you had frostbite and what year you got it, on which toe. Then she could give you ideas on how to work with an illness so that it would not be such a burden. As I began to develop my gift, she helped me learn the disciplines of staying clear, and clean, and rested, and centered. She understood very well that my gift was different from hers. While I needed help, I also needed a wide, open horizon to learn how to proceed on my own. I have been asked many times to help people with healing gifts to begin their work, to learn disciplines, and come to accept what is the particular groove that they are in, that they need to explore and take ownership of.

I'm very happy to do that. I'm always looking for that balance - I point out some things that I think you should be considering and watching for, but you are always going to know the best answers for your work and you are always going to know the lesson that it's teaching you. I'm not going to be a teacher so much as I'm going to help you shape the best questions. What do you think, Elizabeth?

E: A long time ago someone said to me, "Will you be my mentor?" And my answer was, "No, but I will be your friend." And it seemed to me that on the basis of friendship and equality we could share. I don't want to be in the position of telling other people what to believe and what to do. But I'm willing to have a conversation with another person on the basis of that person having something to share with me, too. That may not be a satisfactory answer, but that's still my basis. I feel that I can learn from anyone. That everyone has something that they can share with me. It doesn't have to be a one-way street.

J: Wonderful. Thank you.

① rest
Doing & being p. 199 ② seeking spiritual guidance

Shit hits the fan (when) p. 185

Wounding

50329956R00136

Made in the USA
Middletown, DE
25 June 2019